FLY Tying

An Angler's Complete Handbook and Kit

A FIRESIDE BOOK
PUBLISHED BY SIMON & SCHUSTER INC.
New York•London•Toronto•Sydney•Tokyo•Singapore

Fireside
Simon & Schuster Inc.
Rockefeller Center
1230 Avenue of the Americas
New York, New York 10020

Copyright © 1995 by becker&mayer!, Ltd.
Text copyright ©1995 by Steve Probasco
Interior illustrations ©1995 by Sandy Haight

Cover photo by Burton McNeely/The Image Bank
Interior photos by Roger Schreiber
Photo insets by Steve Probasco
The Art of Fly Tying is produced by becker&mayer!, Ltd.
From *The Art of Fly Tying* packaged set, which includes fly-tying materials, tools, and this book.
All rights reserved including the right of reproduction in whole or in part in any form.

Library of Congress Cataloging-in-Publication Data:

Probasco, Steve
The Art of Fly Tying: An angler's complete handbook and kit / [Steve Probasco]
p. cm.
Includes bibliographical references.
ISBN 0-684-80067-5 (pbk.)
1. Fly Tying I. Title
SH451.P76 1996
688.7'912--dc20 95-44024
CIP

FIRESIDE and colophons are registered trademarks of
Simon & Schuster Inc.

Design/ Electronic Production by Leandra Jones
Package Design/ Illustration by Ani Rucki
Printed in Canada by Solisco Imprimeurs

10 9 8 7 6 5 4 3 2 1

CONTENTS

Introduction

Nearly everyone who fly-fishes will, at one point, get the urge to tie his or her own flies. There is great satisfaction in catching fish with flies you tied yourself. And tying your own will save you plenty of money—in a hurry! In addition, fly tying is just plain fun—hours on end can be spent creating at the fly desk.

In fly-fishing you are not limited to any particular species. There are lines and fly patterns that let us fish for just about anything that swims. In general, we tie flies to imitate the naturally occurring foods of fish. Regardless of what species you are after, flies can be tied that exactly imitate, or generally emulate, its food. From aquatic insects, terrestrial (land-born) insects, and bait fish to frogs and mice—fish eat a wide variety of available foods, and the flytier, with a little practice, can duplicate any of them.

In addition to the flies that imitate the natural food items of fish, there are some flies, called attractors, that don't really imitate anything; rather, with their movement, flash, or color, they entice fish into striking. Attractors are, at times, very important to the fly-fisher.

By reading this book and using the basic kit materials provided, you will learn how to tie five basic flies for trout and panfish: the Woolly Bugger, Dragonfly Nymph, Carey Special, Pheasant Tail Nymph, and Peacock Soft Hackle. Moreover, with the skills you learn by tying the flies featured in this book, you will be able to tie hundreds of standard patterns, as well as create your own flies for trout, panfish, or any other fish. All of the skills you use in tying the five flies featured in this book will be used whenever you tie flies.

In addition to these basic skills, there are many advanced techniques used when tying

more complicated patterns or patterns using different materials than those required by the flies in this book. Once you master basic skills, you will undoubtedly want to learn more; at the end of this book I suggest more advanced tying books.

The step-by-step instruction and photography in this book make learning to tie flies a simple, enjoyable adventure—by the time you finish this book you will be well on your way to becoming a flytier. Each time you create a new fly that fools a fish, the yearning to tie increases. So with that, I say: Belly up to the vise, and happy tying!

©Steve Probasco

Rainbow trout can be taken with any of the flies tied using this kit.

Entomology

The study, classification, and collection of insects is called entomology. Aquatic entomology (the study of water-born insects) is very important to the fly-fisher. Only a handful of aquatic insects concern the angler; the successful fly-fisher must be cognizant of these insects, their life cycles, availability, and fish appeal.

Trout, like most other fish, are opportunistic feeders. They feed on nearly any food item in abundance, although they prefer some insects and food items over others. The major aquatic insects are mayflies, stone flies, caddis flies, dragonflies, damselflies, and midges. Also important are the terrestrials, such as ants, beetles, grasshoppers, and inchworms.

Also of major importance to the trout and the trout fly-fisher are foods such as leeches, crustaceans, snails, other fish, and worms.

In general, knowledge of the basic food items of trout—their size, shape, color, and movement—is a starting point for tying flies that imitate these basic foods. It is important to keep in mind that these food items come in a variety of sizes, and that the trout will often key in on one particular size. This is especially true with aquatic insects.

Understanding the life cycle of the aquatic insects is very important to the fly-fisher. The various stages not only look different, but move differently in the water. For example, some aquatic insects, like the caddis fly, undergo complete metamorphosis: egg to larva to pupa to adult. The successful fly-fisher will understand the basic shape, color, and movement of each stage.

A good way to begin understanding aquatic insects is to go out and actually collect them.

Subaquatic forms can be collected from a stream by holding a piece of door screening attached to dowels crossways in the stream, while scuffing the streambed upstream with your feet. Dislodged insects will float into the screen, where they can be removed from the stream and analyzed. Floating insects can also be caught with a small aquarium screen. Insects in still waters can be collected around shallow shorelines using a small net. Flying insects can be nabbed with your hat.

It is important not only to observe the size, shape, and color of these insects, but also to note their movement in the water. Place the captured specimens in a calm, shallow area and watch how they swim or crawl.

Imitating this movement will be as important to successful fishing as selecting the right size and color of fly.

Once you have a general understanding of the aquatic insects and other food items available to the trout, tying flies to imitate them will be much easier. For a basic reference, here are a few characteristics of the major aquatic food items of the trout.

Mayflies

Mayflies are found in both moving and still waters. The nymph lives in the water for approximately one year. Mayfly nymphs are a major food item of the trout, and imitations are of great importance to the fly-fisher.

There are several varieties of mayflies, but the nymph of most mayflies can be imitated with very basic nymph patterns, such as the PHEASANT TAIL NYMPH featured in this book. Most nymphs are brownish in color.

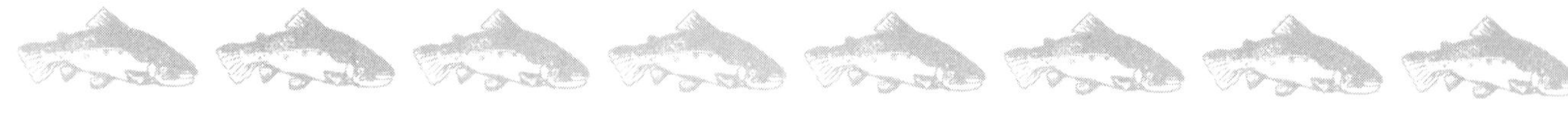

As the nymphs increase in size, they molt (shed their skins) several times. Just before emergence, the adult forms inside the nymphal shuck. The wing pads enlarge and grow dark in color. It then swims to the surface, where the dun hatches. Duns are usually drab in color.

While sitting on the water, they hold their wings high, like tiny sailboats. One day later the dun molts to become the sexually mature spinner. Spinners have glossy bodies and clear wings. They can be found in several colors.

The spinners fall onto the water to lay eggs, and their wings fall to their sides, causing them to resemble an airplane.

Stone Flies

The nymph lives in highly oxygenated, moving water for one or two years. Nymphs can be large—up to a couple of inches in length. Most are dark brown to black on the back, slightly lighter on the underside.

When ready to hatch into the adult stage, the nymph crawls to shore and the adult emerges, usually at night. The WOOLLY BUGGER featured in this book could be mistaken for a stone fly nymph when fished in fast-moving streams.

The adults vary in color with species. Yellow, orange, gray, rust, and brown are common colors. The female lands on the water to lay eggs, and this usually causes an all-out feeding frenzy.

Caddis Flies

The larva lives in the water for one year. It then seals itself in a case on the stream's bottom and becomes a pupa. After a few weeks the pupa

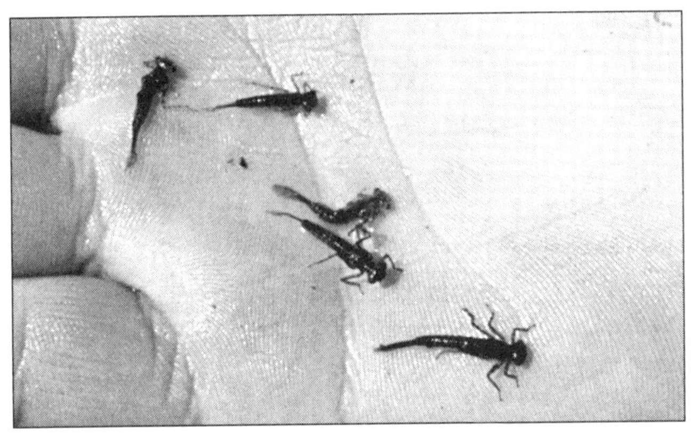

cuts free of the case and swims to the surface, where the adult emerges. Pupas range in color from tan to green to brown to rust. During this emergence the caddis fly is in great peril. Soft-hackled flies like the PEACOCK SOFT HACKLE featured in this book are highly effective during the emergence. Females land on the water to lay eggs.

Damselflies/Dragonflies

Nymphs live in the water for one or two years. Although similiar in appearance, the dragonfly nymphs are much larger than the damselflies. Mature nymphs swim (damselflies) or crawl (dragonflies) to land, and then the adult emerges. It is during emergence that both nymphs are most vulnerable. Both nymphs present in shades of green and brown.

The dragonfly nymph is realistically imitated with the DRAGONFLY NYMPH featured in this book. The damselfly nymph can be emulated with both the CAREY SPECIAL and the PEACOCK SOFT HACKLE when tied in small sizes.

Although female damselflies and dragonflies deposit eggs on the water, the adults are not as important as the nymphs.

Midges

The larval stage lives up to a few months. The pupa is free-swimming and moves up and down in the water column. The pupal stage is very important to the fly-fisher, as it is available in great numbers all year long. They are found in a variety of dull earth tones, but black is the most prevalent. Adults emerge at the surface, and females return to the water to lay their eggs on the surface.

Leeches

Most leeches live near the bottom. They may reproduce several times per year. Trout love leeches. Shades of brown, green, and black are most common. The WOOLLY BUGGER is a very good leech imitation.

Scuds

These freshwater shrimp live in shallows, down to 10 feet. Wherever you find scuds, you will find a healthy population of trout, as they are a favorite food. A small, soft-hackled fly like the PEACOCK SOFT HACKLE will do a fair job of imitating these erratic swimmers.

Snails

Trout feed actively on small snails that live in shallows and in weed beds. Again, tied in the appropriate size, the PEACOCK SOFT HACKLE does a fair job of imitating a snail.

Food Fishes

Usually found in weedbeds and shallows. Trout will eat other fish, and some of the larger fish in the river or lake will take minnow imitations.

©Steve Probasco

Knowing the natural food a fish eats is essential to choosing the right fly.

Tools and Materials

The modern flytier has a myriad of tools and tying materials from which to choose. New tools and fly patterns are constantly being developed, and the flytier of today needs to stay aware of what's available.

In this section, I mention only a few of the common tools and materials in use. It would be impossible to name every tool and material used in fly tying, as the list would be a mile long. Use this section as a general guide when selecting tools and materials. Don't be afraid to experiment and try new things on your own. Who knows, you may come up with a revolutionary new material or tool that makes some technique easier.

This beginning kit is limited in the tools and materials provided. The intention is simply to introduce you to the art of fly tying, with tools and materials provided to tie five basic patterns.

Tools

Your tying tools are very important. From the basic tools, such as those included in this kit—vise, bobbin, hackle pliers, and whip finisher—to the specialized tools needed for more advanced fly tying, your tools make certain aspects of fly tying much easier.

Materials

The list of body materials available to the flytier is endless. The most common items used are floss, chenille, wool, spun fur, and several synthetic materials, which come wound on small cards.

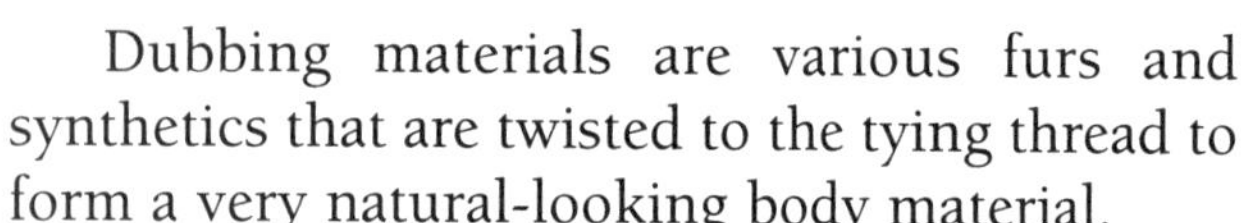

Dubbing materials are various furs and synthetics that are twisted to the tying thread to form a very natural-looking body material.

Many different types of feathers, hairs, tails, and synthetics are used in fly tying, creating everything from wings and tails to legs and antennas of various insects.

Using this kit, you will be able to tie five flies using these few materials: marabou (one fuzzy olive feather), saddle hackle (six dark olive feathers), pheasant rump feathers (three), chenille, pheasant tail, peacock herl (twenty strands), copper wire, and black thread.

Following are close-ups of the tools and materials you will be using—you should refer back to these photos as you tie.

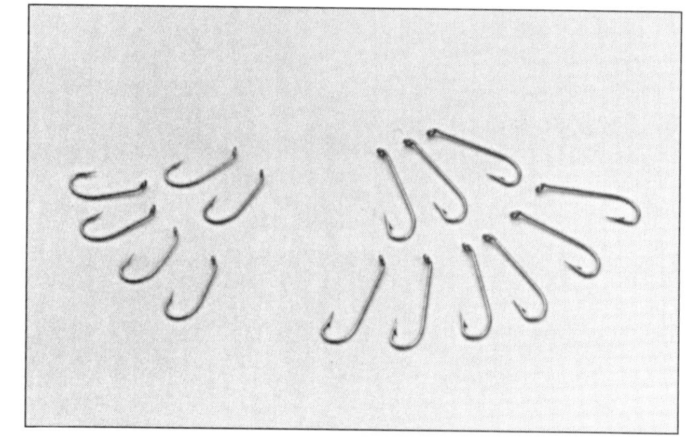

Hooks: In this kit there are two different sizes of hooks. The long hooks will be used for tying the Woolly Bugger, Dragonfly Nymph, and Carey Special. The short hooks will be used for the Pheasant Tail Nymph and Peacock Soft Hackle.

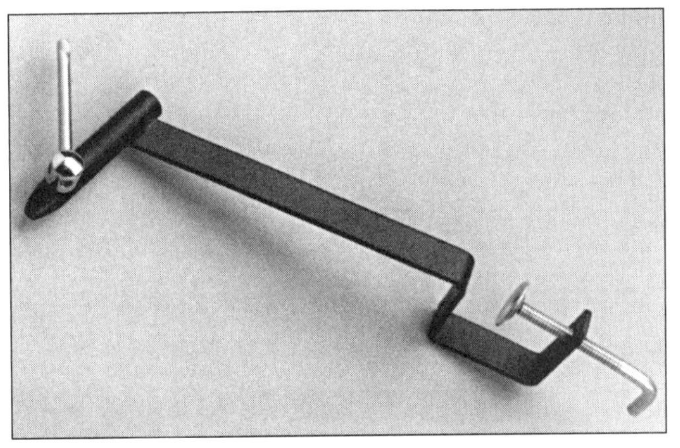

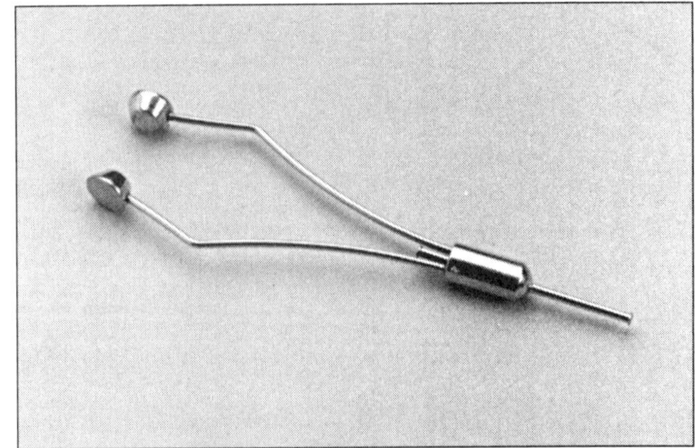

Vise: The most important tool in any fly tying kit is the vise that holds the hook during the tying process.

Bobbin: The bobbin holds your tying thread and keeps it under constant tension.

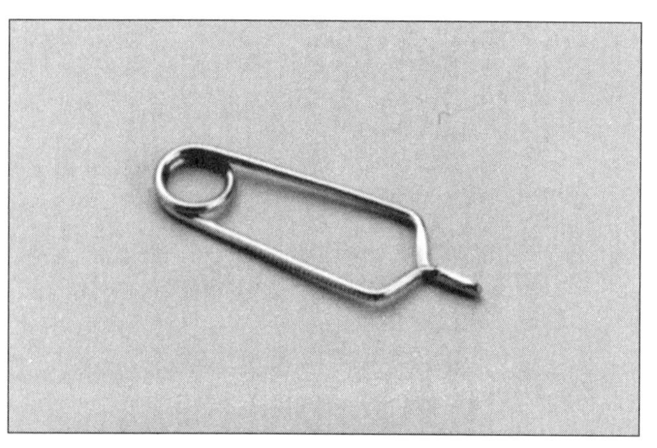

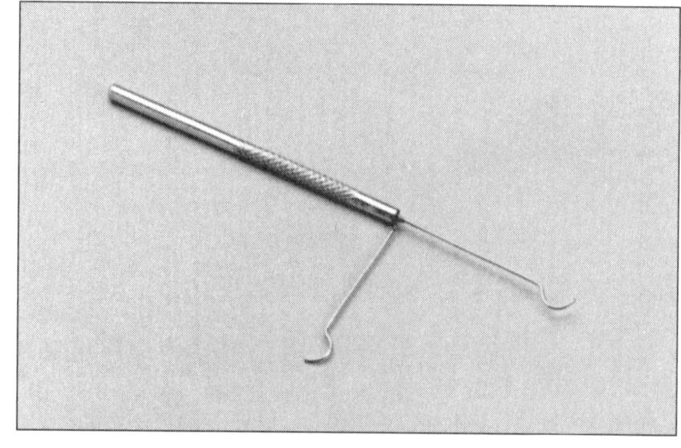

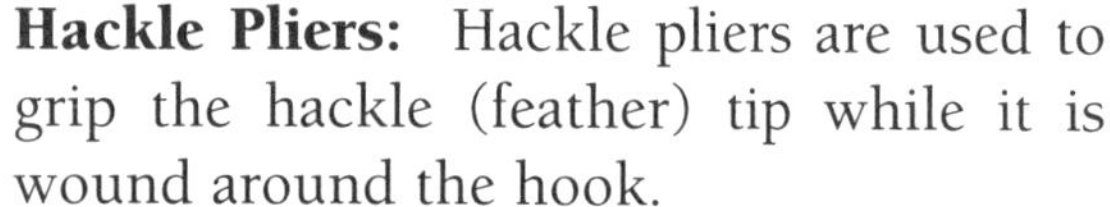

Hackle Pliers: Hackle pliers are used to grip the hackle (feather) tip while it is wound around the hook.

Whip Finisher: This tool allows you to tie a knot rapidly, securing the thread at the head of the fly.

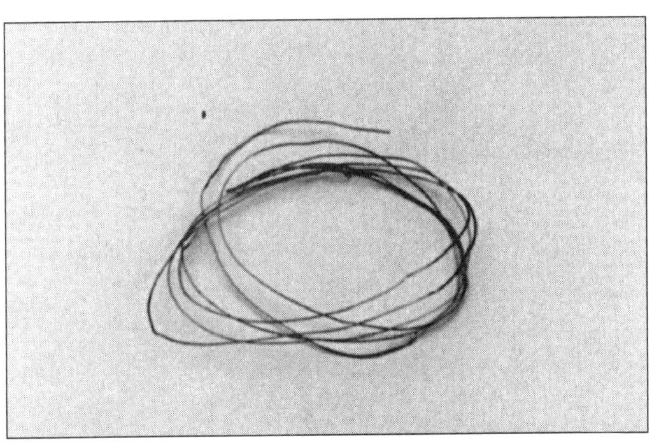

Copper Wire: The copper wire is used for the ribbing on both the PHEASANT TAIL NYMPH and PEACOCK SOFT HACKLE.

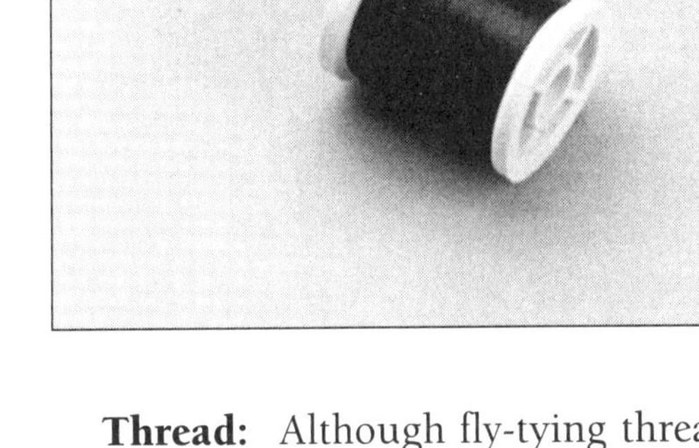

Thread: Although fly-tying thread comes in a variety of colors and sizes, the black thread included in this kit is useful for a variety of flies.

Pheasant Rump Feather: This rust-colored rump feather will be used as the hackle on the CAREY SPECIAL.

Saddle Hackle: The olive-colored saddle hackle will be wound on the WOOLLY BUGGER, DRAGONFLY NYMPH, and PEACOCK SOFT HACKLE.

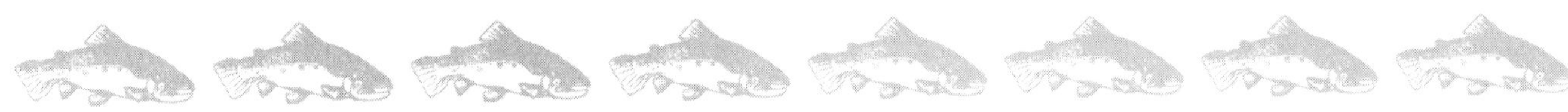

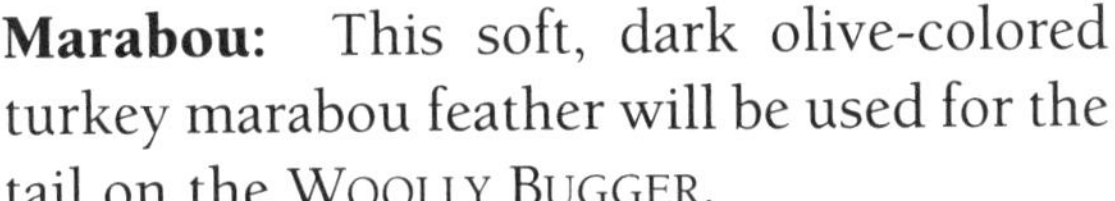

Marabou: This soft, dark olive-colored turkey marabou feather will be used for the tail on the WOOLLY BUGGER.

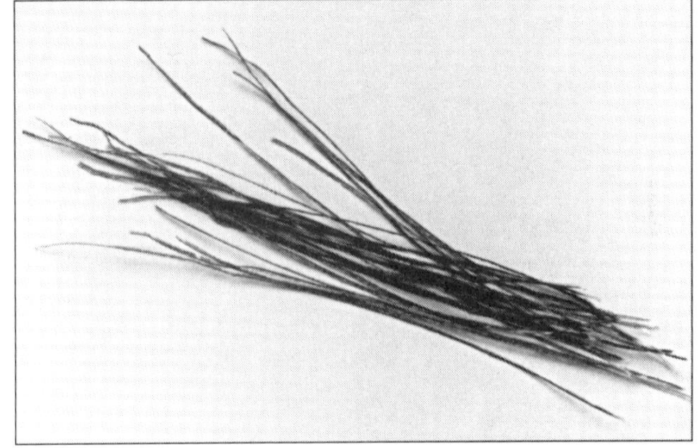

Peacock Herl: Peacock herl will be used to form the body of the PEACOCK SOFT HACKLE and the thorax of the PHEASANT TAIL NYMPH.

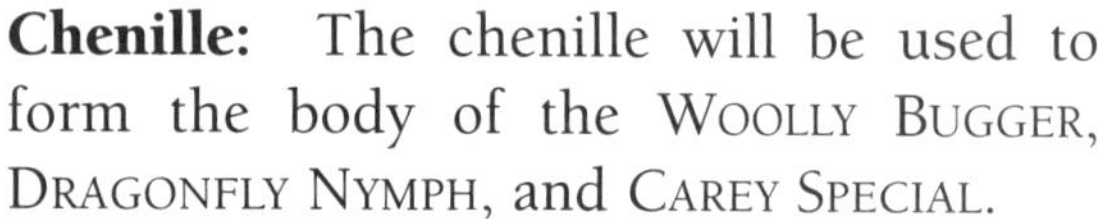

Chenille: The chenille will be used to form the body of the Woolly Bugger, Dragonfly Nymph, and Carey Special.

Pheasant Tail: This pheasant tail will be used to form the tail, abdomen, thorax, and legs of the Pheasant Tail Nymph.

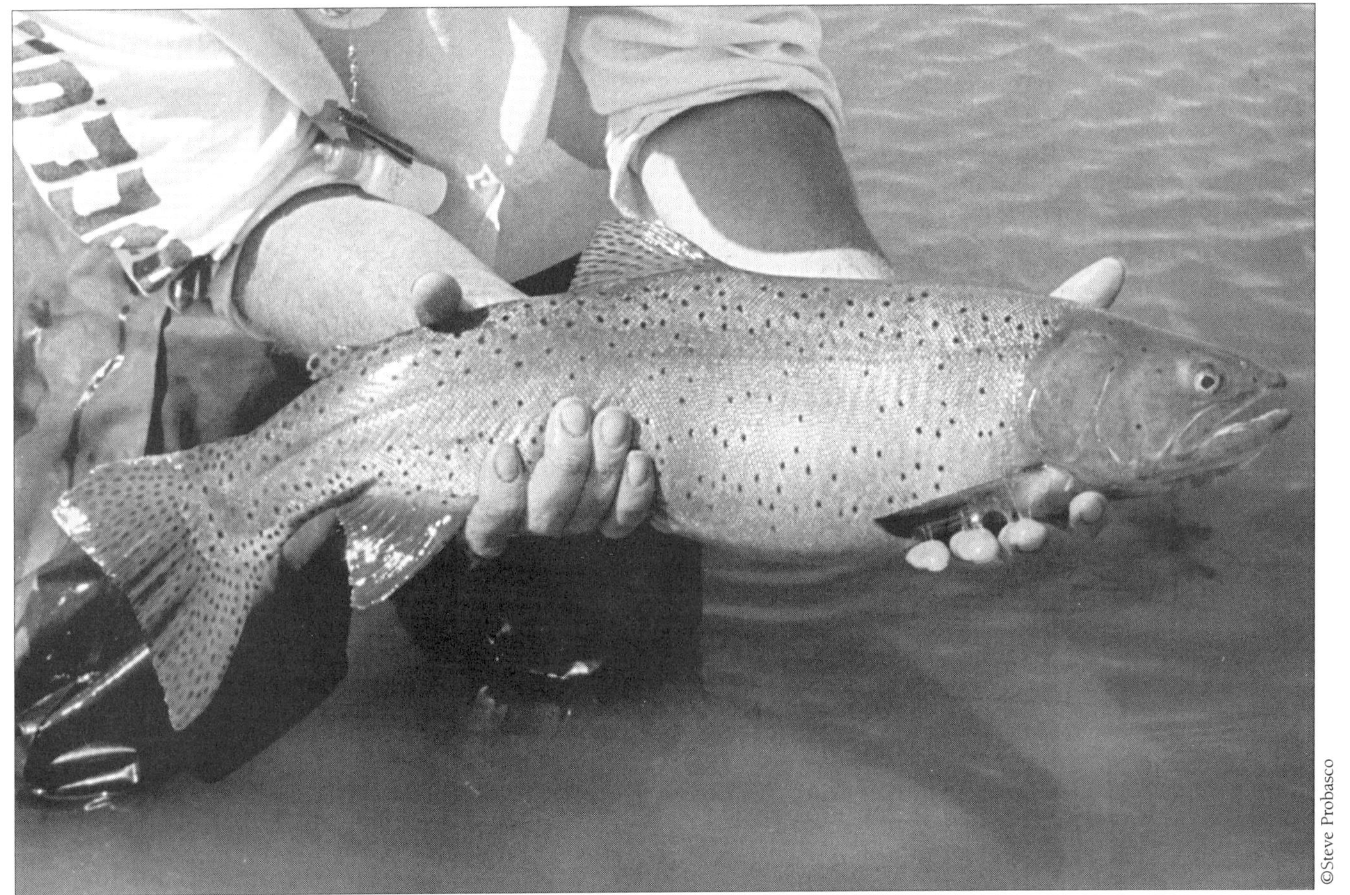

©Steve Probasco

Large Lahonton cut-throat trout from Grimes Lake, Washington.

Other Useful Tools

Besides the tools included in this kit, you will eventually upgrade and add to your collection. Here is a list of a few other useful tools.

Hair Stacker: When you're tying with hair, this is an invaluable tool. Its job is to align the hair tips before tying onto the hook.

Scissors: Fine-point scissors are a must for all delicate work.

Bodkin: This tool is used for applying head cement and picking out dubbing fur.

Monofilament Line: 50-pound-test monofilament line is used to make the eyes of the Dragonfly Nymph.

Bobbin Threader: Using this inexpensive tool is another way to thread the bobbin.

Material Holder: This spring clip attaches to the vise just behind the jaws to hold long materials out of your way.

Dubbing Twister: This tool will help you to make thick fur bodies.

Head Cement: Although not mandatory, head cement will make the head of your finished fly much more durable.

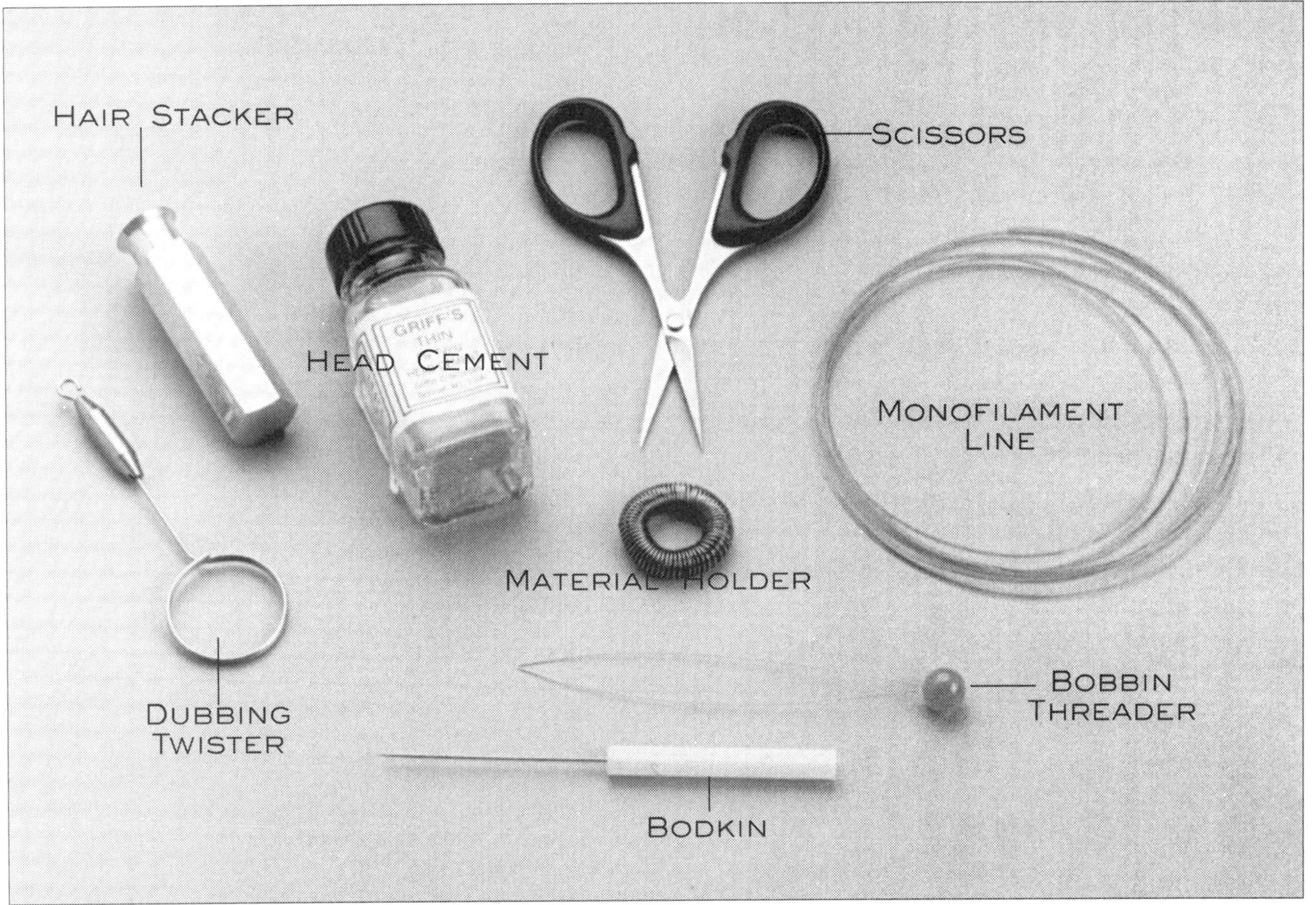
Hair Stacker
Scissors
Head Cement
Monofilament Line
Material Holder
Bobbin Threader
Dubbing Twister
Bodkin

Basic Techniques

There are a few basic techniques you should be familiar with before attempting to tie any of the flies in this book. Some involve the tying tools and their proper use. Although none of these techniques are difficult, learning them beforehand will certainly make tying the flies more enjoyable—and as simple as following a recipe. Each fly calls for different materials to be tied onto the hook in a variety of ways. Practice these techniques by using the specific materials called for in the instructions for tying any one fly, or improvise, using the materials on hand.

The number one difficulty for beginners is making materials end properly so that a small, neat head can be tied. Keep this in mind as this step draws near on each fly.

Practice the techniques shown on a bare hook until they are easy. Then it will be time to tie your first fly.

Follow the step-by-step instructions, and look closely at the photographs of each step. If your fly doesn't look like the ones pictured at each step—STOP and correct it. Keep repeating that step until it looks right, and remember what you needed to do to make it right.

This will be valuable information down the line. Finally, have fun and be creative. Fly tying is a wonderful way to save money as well as pass the time.

The Vise

A fly-tying vise simply holds the hook. It must hold a wide range of hook sizes firmly and tighten easily.

Attach vise to table edge. Turn the handle clockwise until the jaws open, insert the hook as shown, just to barb, and rotate the handle counterclockwise until the hook is held tight. Test by pulling on the hook with your fingers.

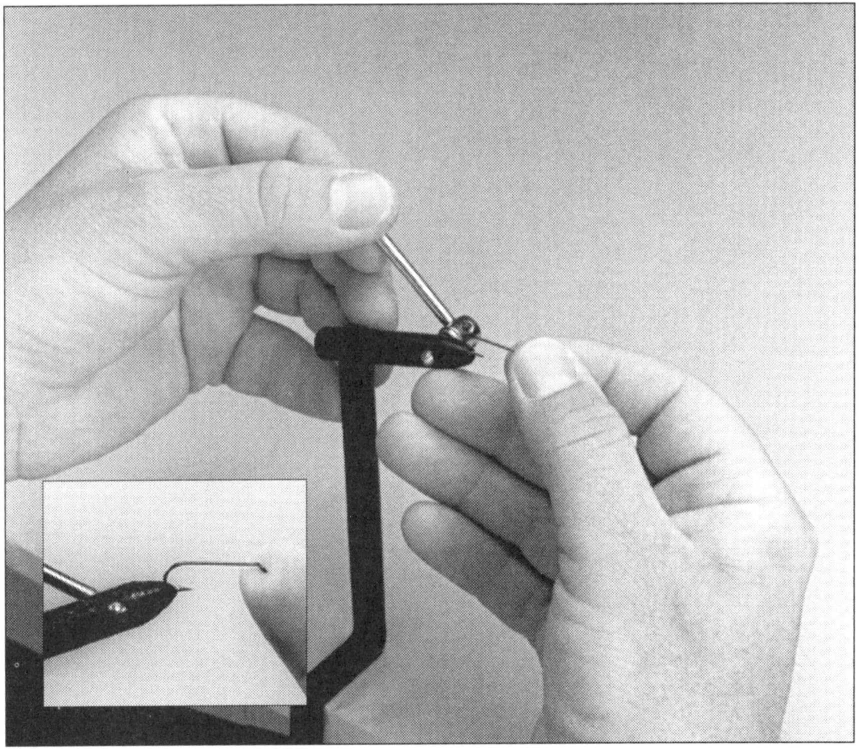

The Bobbin

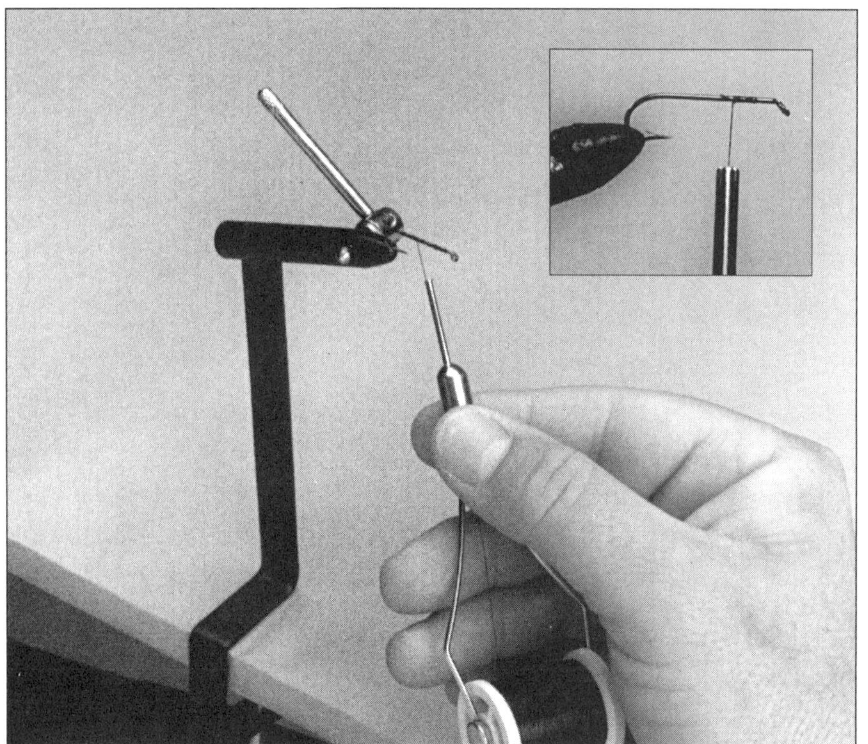

Place thread spool between the arms of the bobbin. If tension doesn't allow thread to pull off evenly, remove spool, stretch arms slightly, and reinsert spool.

Pull a strand of thread out from spool, insert it into the tube, and suck it through the other side.

Secure materials to the hook by revolving the bobbin around the shank, wrapping the thread tightly. The hanging bobbin keeps tension on your tying thread when you are not using it to wrap on materials. Keep the thread between hook and bobbin short enough to allow bobbin to hang fully suspended.

The Hackle Pliers

Hackle pliers clamp onto the tip of a feather segment to make it easy to wind that feather around a hook.

Squeeze the pliers, fully opening the jaws. Place the feather tip into the pliers and release tension.

The weight of the hackle pliers will hold tension on the feather and make it easy to wind.

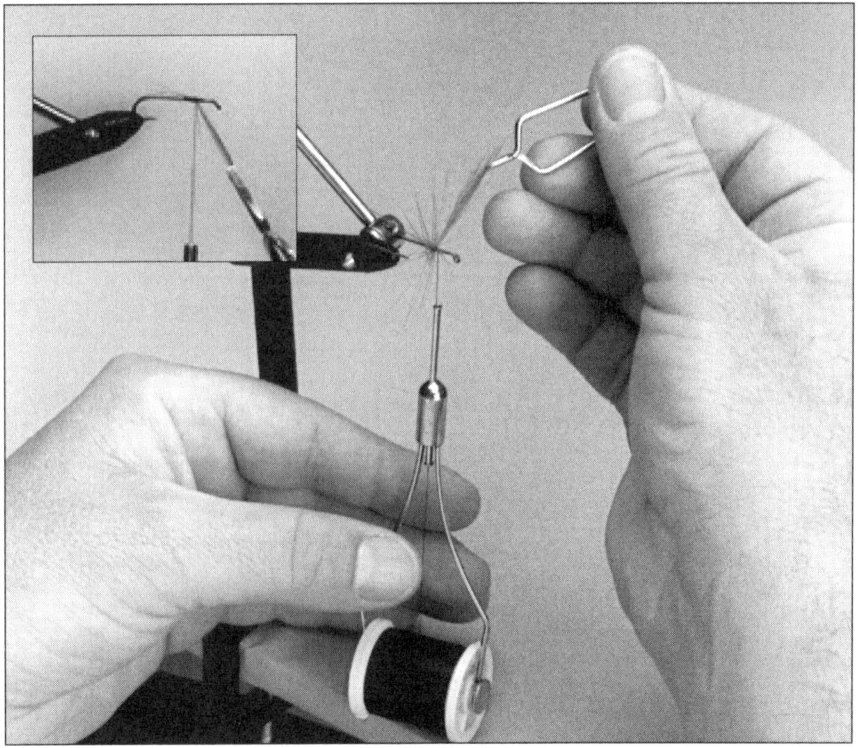

Covering the Hook Shank

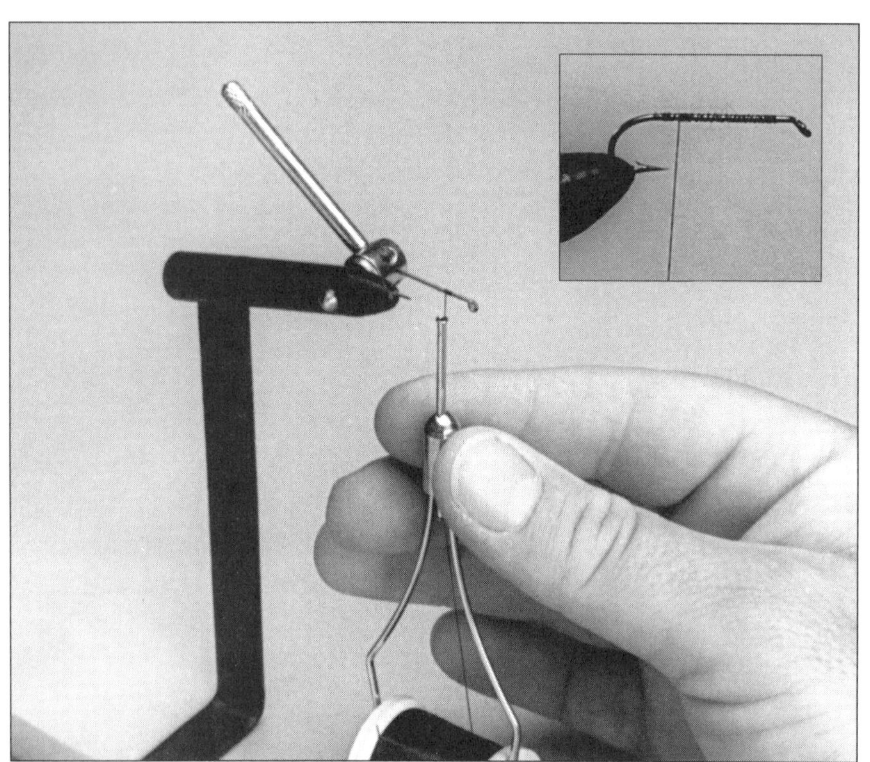

Before tying on any body materials, cover the hook shank with tying thread.

Secure thread to the hook by laying a length of thread along the hook shank and winding over it, revolving the bobbin up and down the shank over previous wraps of the thread, finishing above the barb.

This will make materials less apt to slip or spin.

The Soft Loop

Use a soft loop to secure materials right on top of the hook shank so they will not roll off to the side.

Hold the materials in place on top of hook shank with thumb and forefinger (see tying instructions for specific materials and instructions). Use bobbin to make a loose loop around the shank and materials. Trap the loop between your thumb and forefinger. With other hand, pull straight down on the tying thread, at the same time slowly releasing the loop to cinch materials in place. Repeat as needed.

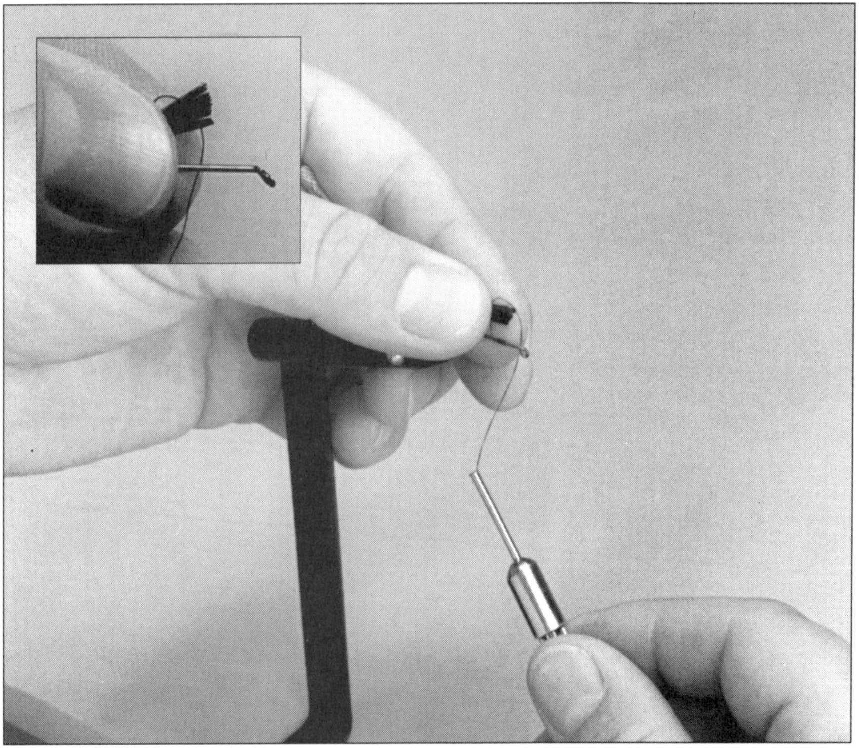

Securing Materials

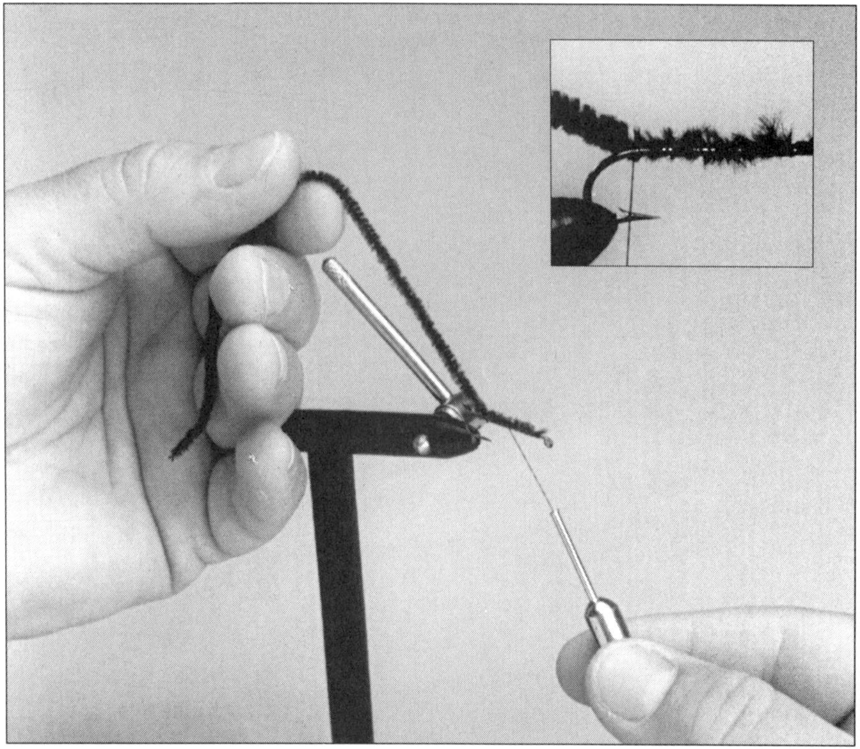

When tying on body materials, secure them the full length of the hook shank by winding the thread clockwise up and down the body, per instructions for each specific fly.

Palmering Hackle

Winding hackle (feathers) up the body of the fly gives the fly authentic movement.

To palmer, or wind, hackle, secure one end of the feather to the hook shank with several wraps of thread just above the barb. Attach hackle pliers to the feather's free end and wind the hackle forward. (See specific instructions to determine which end is tied in first.)

When done winding, secure with several wraps of your tying thread a bit behind the eye of the hook, leaving room to wind on the fly's head.

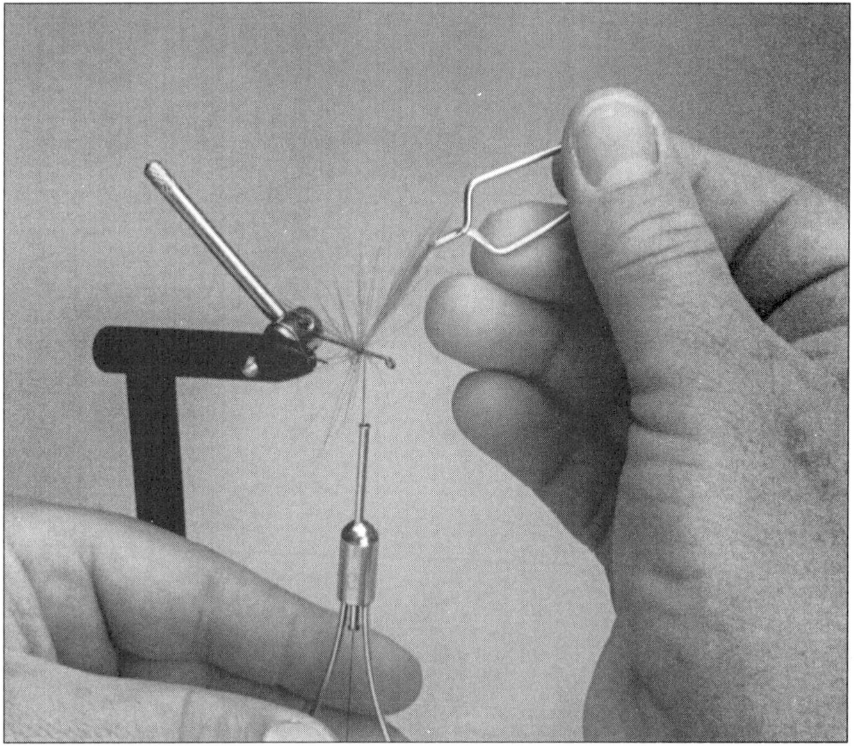

Winding Rib

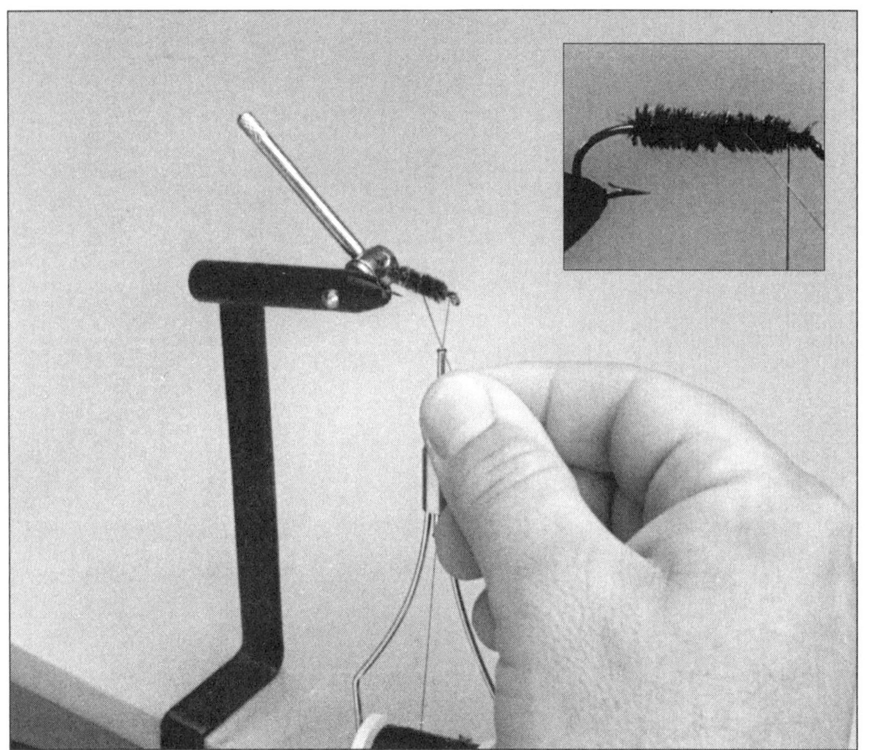

When winding the rib (any material used to create body segments on a fly—copper wire in this kit), always wind it counterclockwise over the body material.

This keeps the rib from sinking out of sight in the turns of the body material, and will better secure your body material.

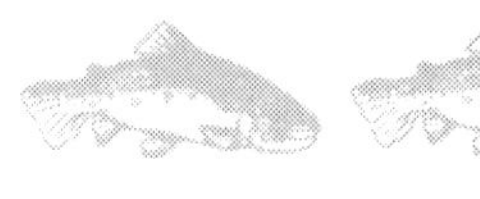

Monofilament Eyes

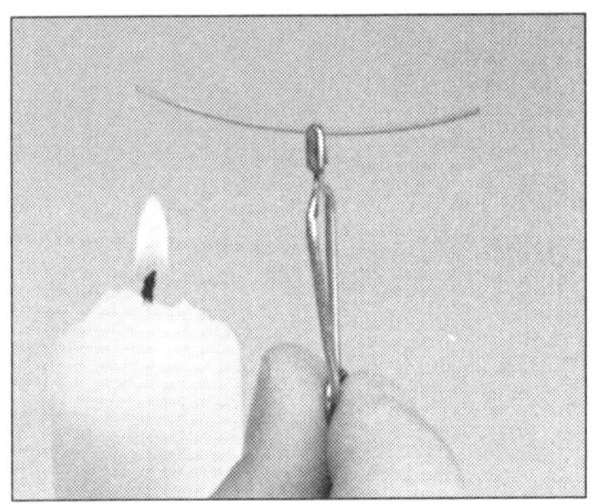

Making eyes of monofilament fishing line is a very effective way to emulate the eyes of large-eyed nymphs, such as the DRAGONFLY NYMPH featured in this book. Note: You may also buy fly eyes inexpensively at fly-fishing specialty stores.

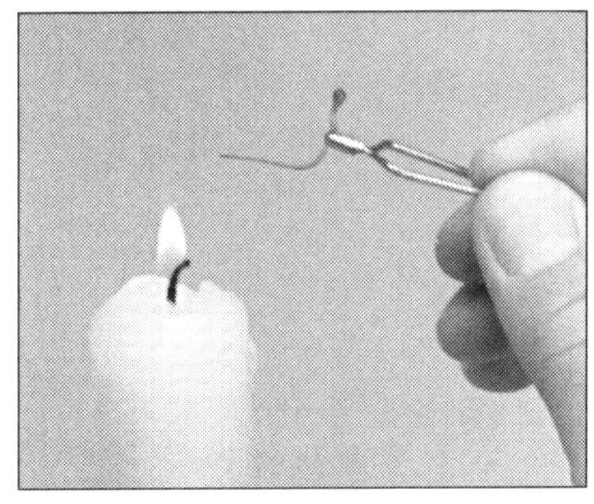

To make the eyes, hold a 2-inch piece of 60-pound-test monofilament in the center with the hackle pliers.

Holding just over the flame of a candle and swiveling constantly in and out of the heat, melt down the ends of the mono to form a ball at either end.

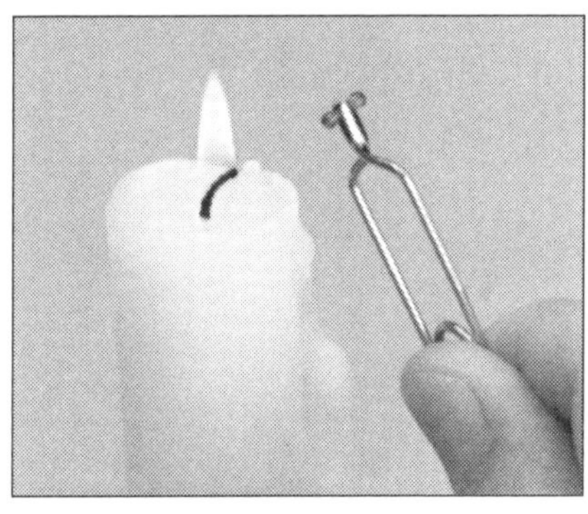

The distance between eyes should be about the width of the pliers, but be careful not to melt them to the pliers.

If line catches fire, blow it out, let cool, and begin again. Be careful handling eyes until they're dry, as the melted line is very hot.

The Whip Finisher

Note: *Many flytiers prefer to finish off their flies with a series of half hitch knots—the simplest of techniques* (see page 38).

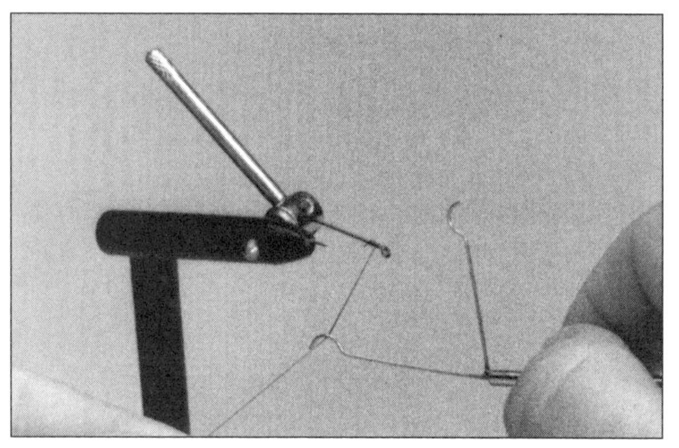

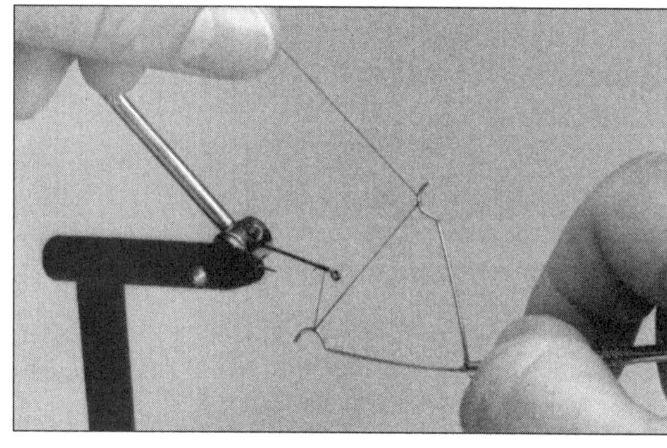

Step 1

To tie a knot securing thread at the head of a fly, leave hook in vise and attach the thread leading off the fly to the whip finisher's lower arm spring, while holding the upper arm vertical.

Step 2

Move thread up and over the vertical arm, hooking it as you go.

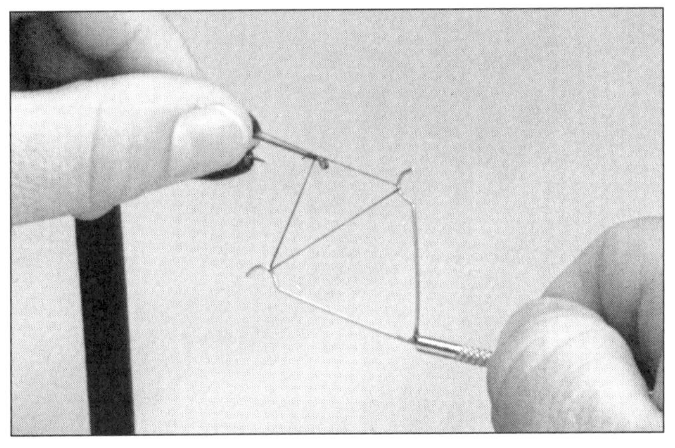

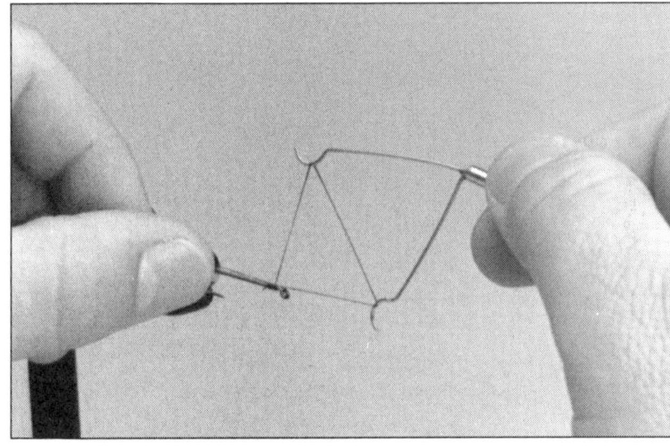

Step 3

Using your left hand, lay the thread along the hook shank.

Step 4

Wind lower arm around the hook shank, pivoting around the upper arm.

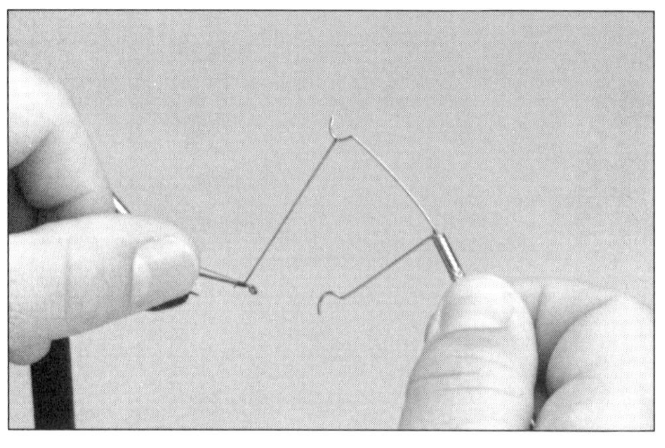

Step 5

Lift one arm up high, keeping tension on the thread with the whip finisher, and unhook the bottom arm from the thread.

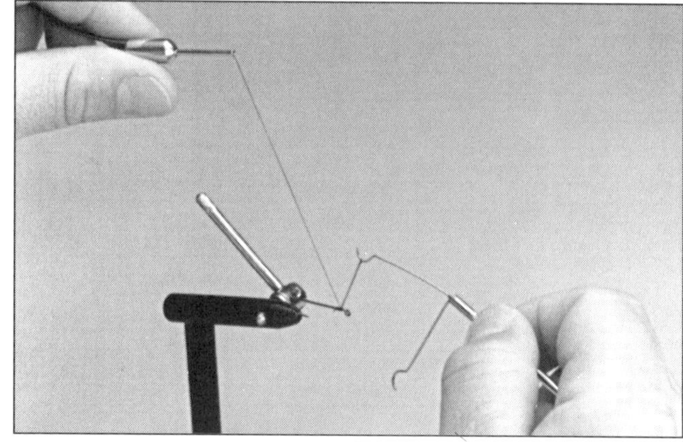

Step 6

Pull thread end attached to bobbin and hook taut with the fingers of your left hand.

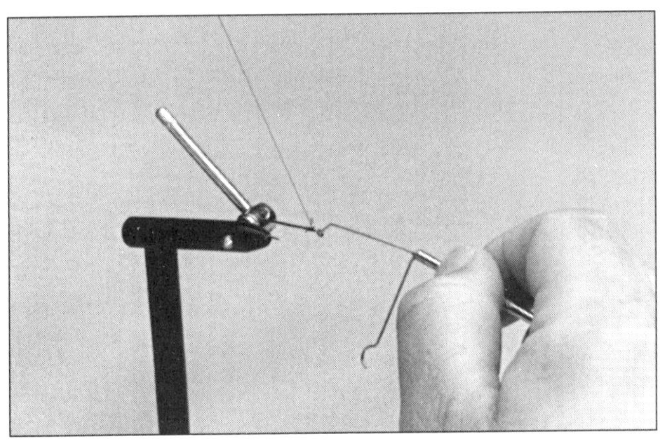

Step 7

Pull thread tight and cinch, slipping the hook of the whip finisher out from the thread.

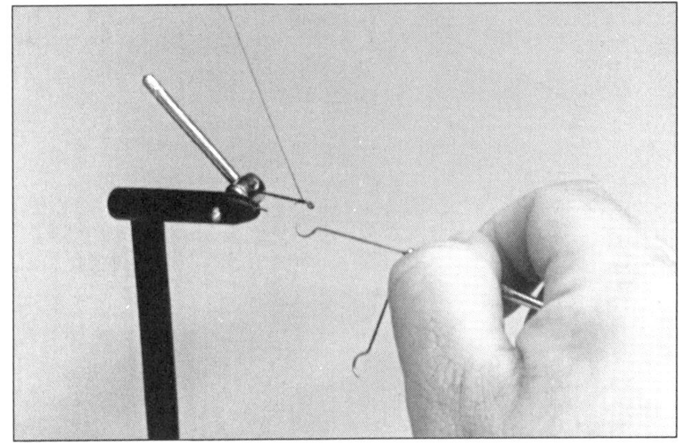

Step 8

Trim close.

The Half Hitch

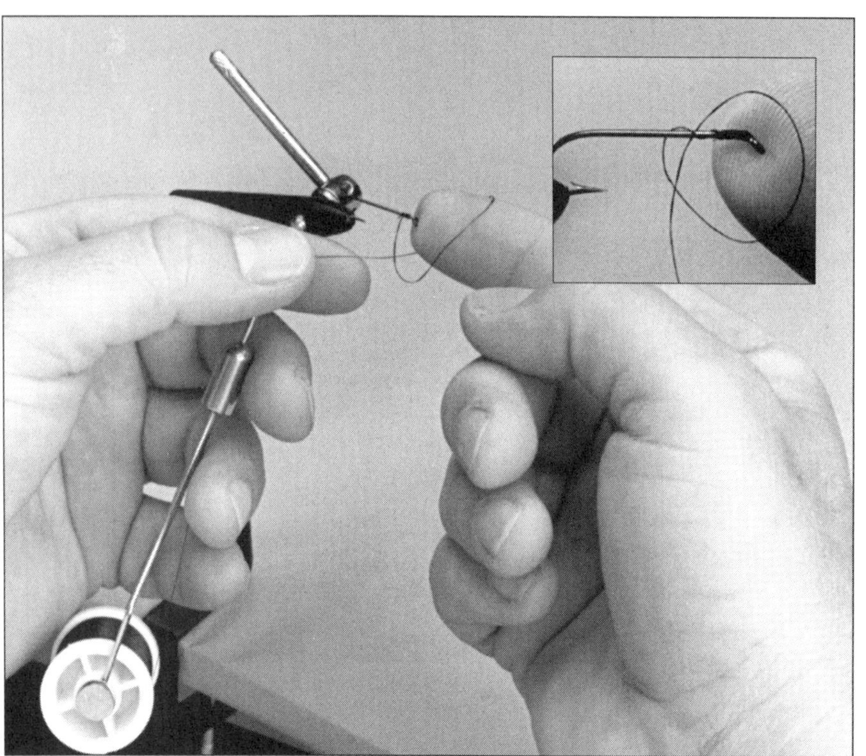

The half hitch is a simple knot used to secure materials to your hook in place of a final whip finish.

To make one, simply make a loop around the end of your fingertip and place that finger to the hook eye. Slip the loop off your finger, cinching it around shank, just behind the eye. Repeat several times to finish off your fly, or place anywhere along the hook shank to secure materials, as needed.

Anatomy of a Fly

Woolly Bugger

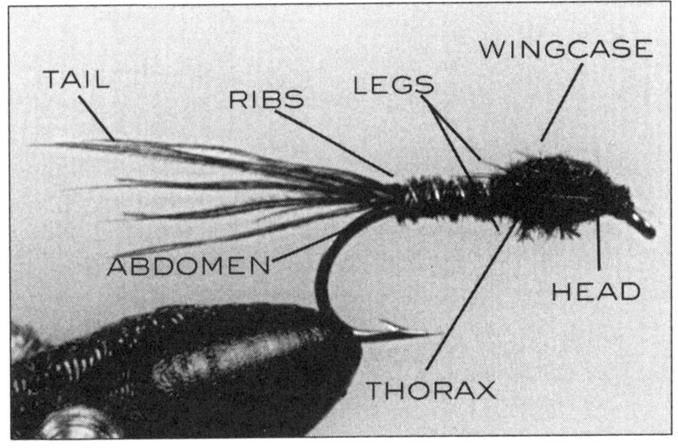

Pheasant Tail Nymph

WOOLLY BUGGER

There is probably no fly more popular for a variety of gamefishes than the Woolly Bugger. This fly has taken nearly every species of fish, in all corners of the world. As a trout fly, the Bugger is hard to beat.

Fish probably most often take the Woolly Bugger as a leech, dragonfly nymph, crayfish, or minnow, depending on the size and color in which it is tied. Fished from the top to the bottom, the Bugger produces in a big way.

Most often the Woolly Bugger is fished on a line that will place it right near the bottom, imitating the leech. Buggers fished on the bottom should be worked very slowly. Short jerks of the line will mimic the movements of a leech inching along.

The Woolly Bugger can be tied in a variety of colors. Black, olive, and brown are three of the most popular hues, but don't overlook red, purple, yellow, and white, as these colors are also effective at times.

This is one of the easiest and most effective patterns you can use for many fish, including trout, panfish, and bass.

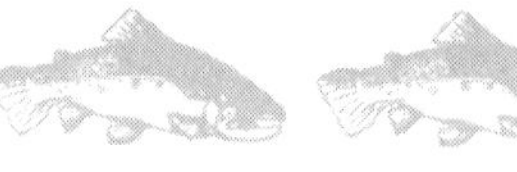

MATERIALS

Hook:	Mustad 33960 (long-shank hook)
Thread:	Black
Body:	Dark olive chenille
Hackle:	Dark olive saddle hackle
Tail:	Olive marabou

Tying Steps

Note: You will find it helpful to refer back to the chapters "Tools and Materials" and "Basic Techniques" as you tie your first flies.

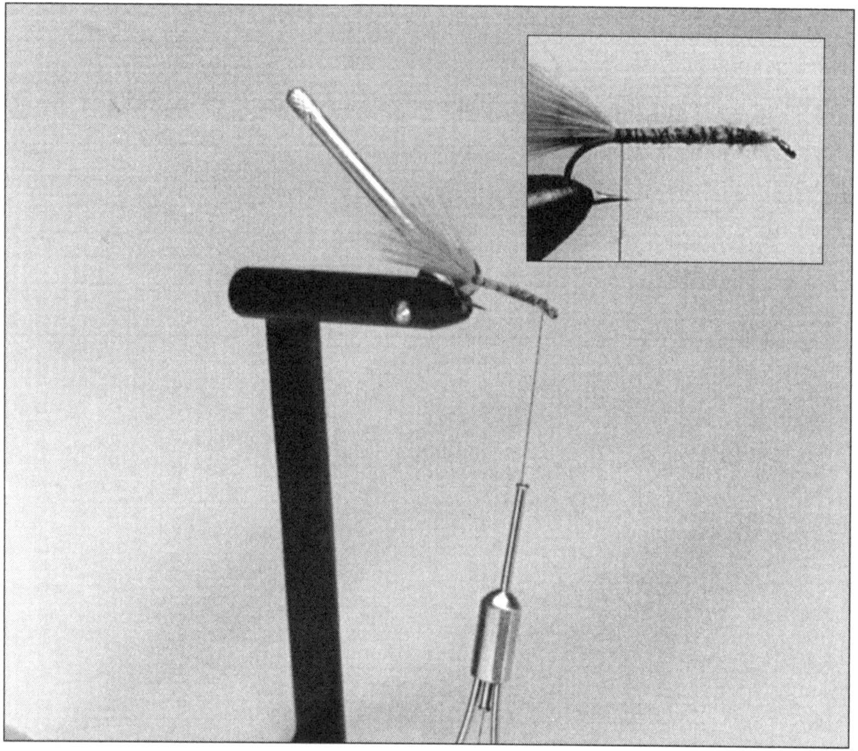

Step 1

Wrap hook shank with thread (see page 28).

Cut off the tip of a turkey marabou feather to a length double that of the hook shank. Lay feather along hook shank, from a bit behind the eye to extend past the bend of the hook, as shown. Secure with a soft loop at eye end, then wrap securely toward tail, to just above the barb. Secure with several wraps and wind back up to a bit behind the eye, leaving room to wrap on a head—about 1/8 inch.

Step 2

Lay a 4-inch piece of olive chenille atop hook shank and hackle, from behind eye to above barb. Secure as in Step 1. Make sure your tying thread ends up directly above the barb of the hook. The extra chenille will hang off to the side at the hook end.

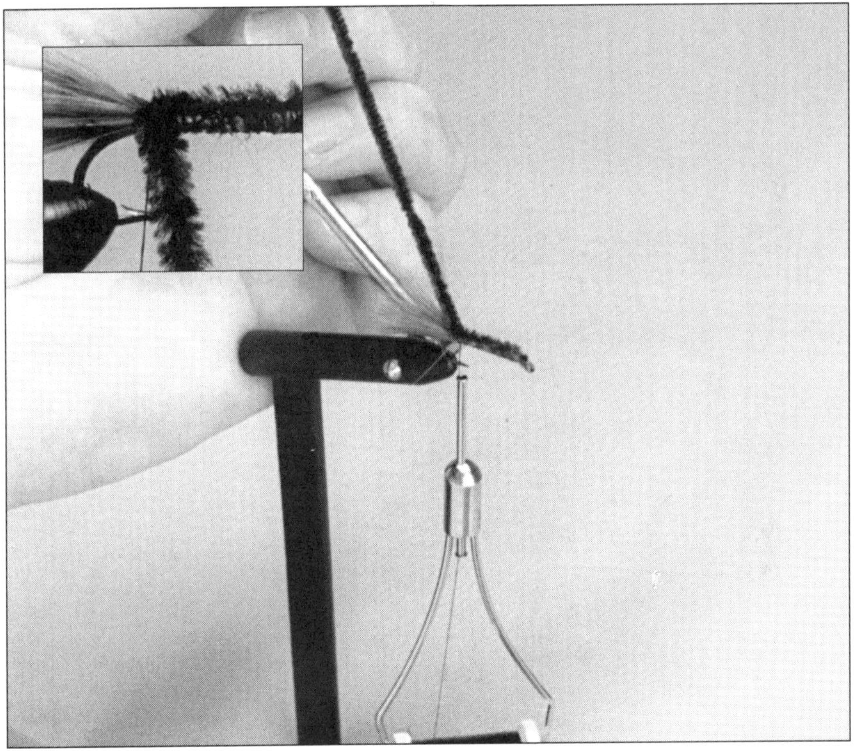

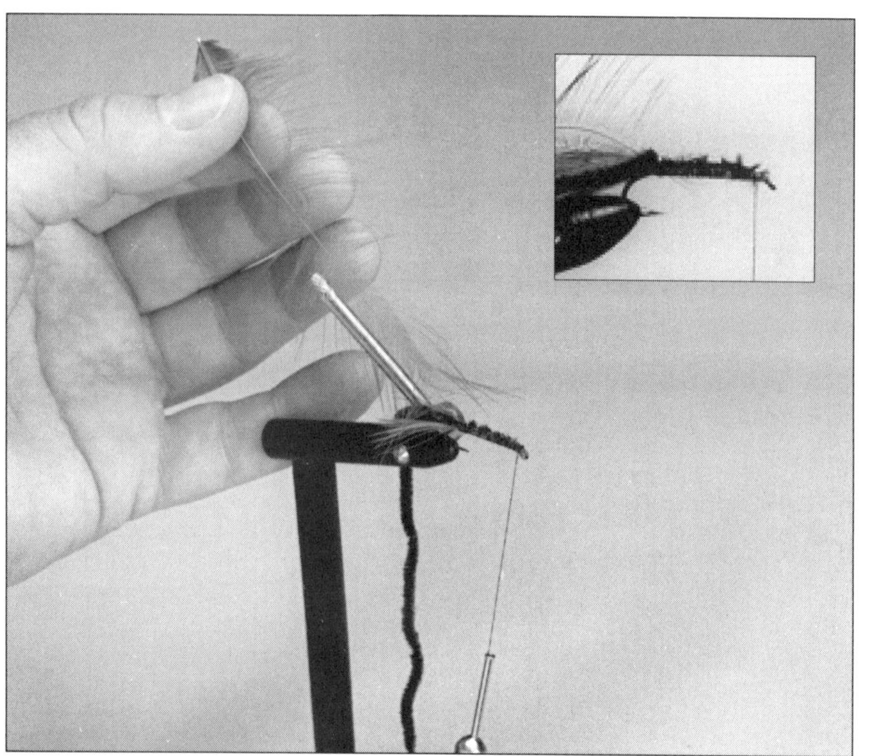

Step 3

Tie in an entire saddle hackle (olive feather, see page 18), using the soft loop method to secure the tip (not the quill end) atop the chenille, a bit behind the hook eye. As with the chenille, wrap the feather tightly with thread to just above the barb, allowing excess to trail behind the hook. Secure with several wraps and wind thread forward to starting point behind eye.

Step 4

Tightly wind chenille body forward in a clockwise direction. Stop the chenille about ⅛ inch from the eye of the hook. Wind over the chenille with the tying thread to secure at the head. Trim excess chenille, being careful not to cut bobbin thread.

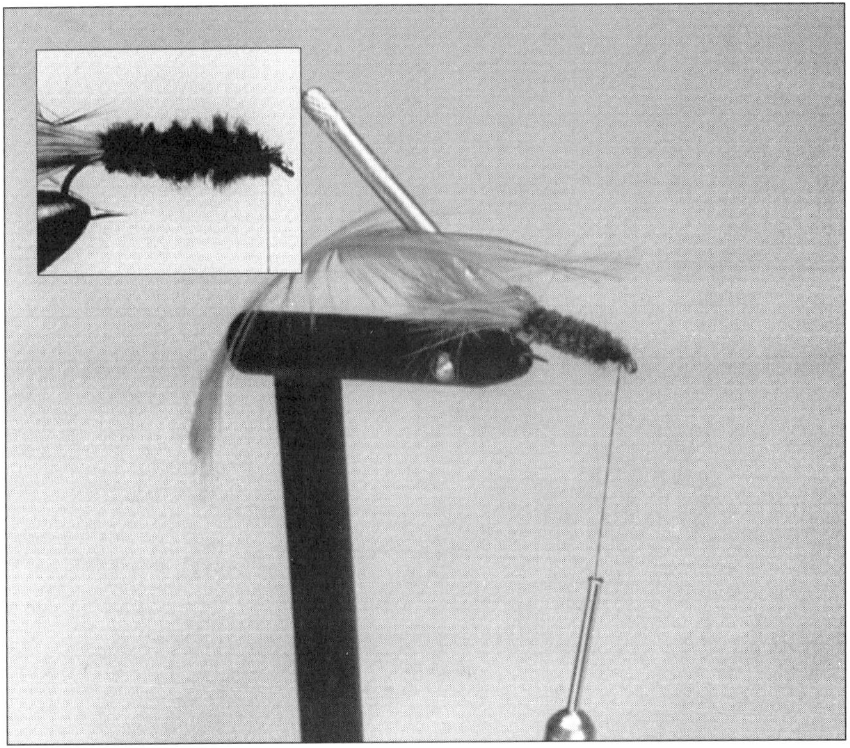

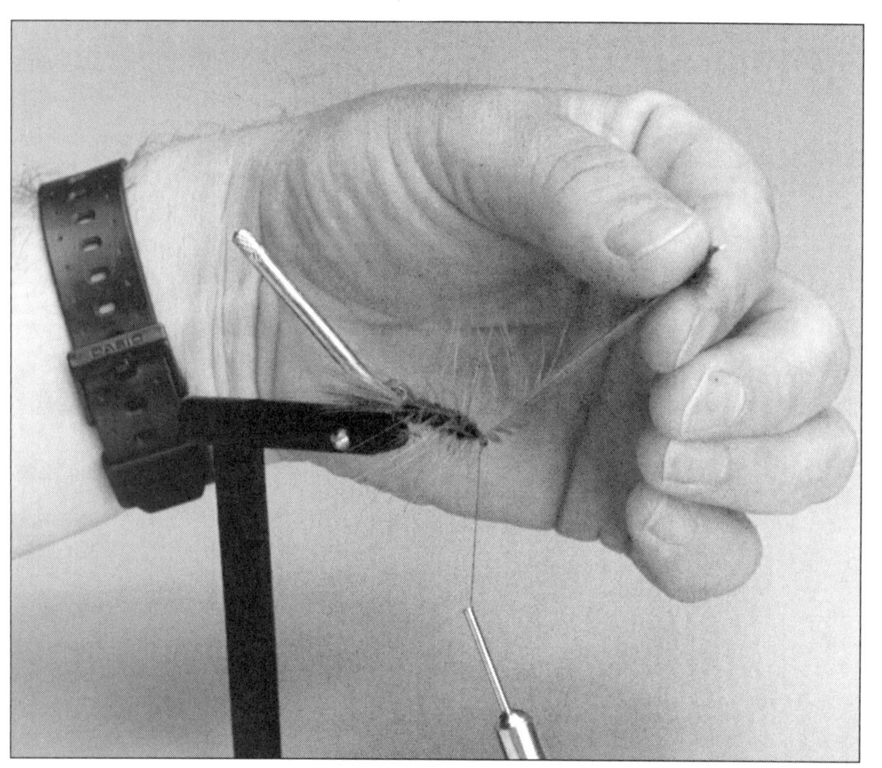

Step 5

Using hackle pliers or fingers, wind the hackle forward, spacing the wraps of the feather so that it extends to the point where you ended winding the chenille, a bit behind the hook eye.

Secure with several wraps of the tying thread at the head end. Carefully trim any excess hackle at head.

Step 6

Pulling hackle fibers back out of the way, use a series of wraps of the thread to create a $^{1}/_{16}$-inch head on your fly between body materials and hook eye.

Finish with the whip finisher technique you learned earlier or three or four half hitches.

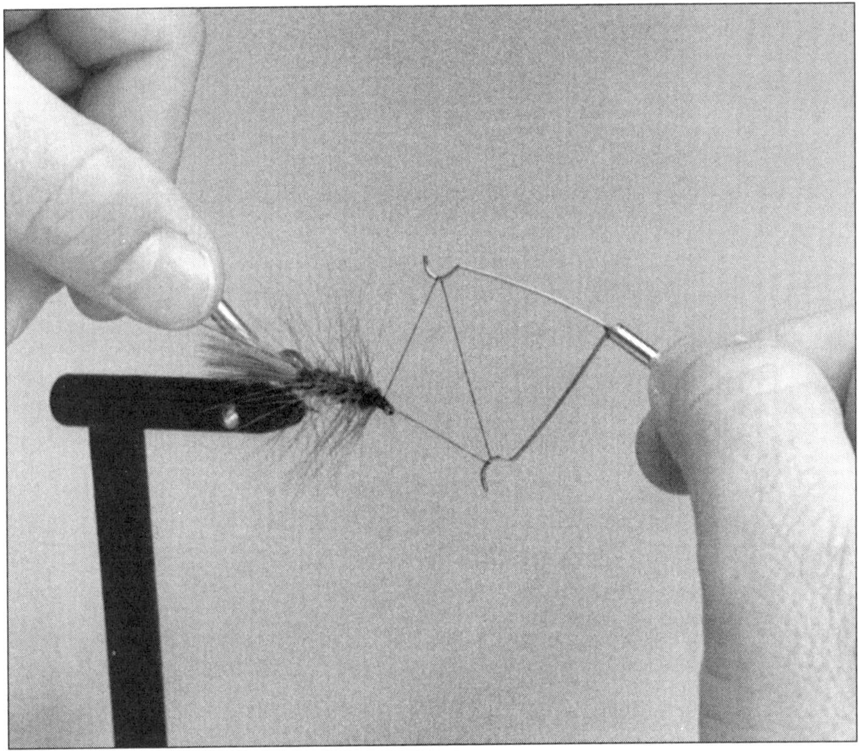

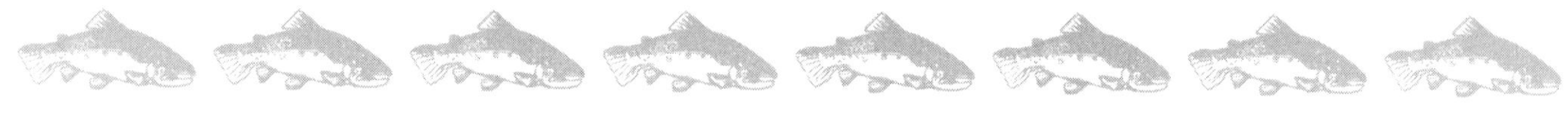

Step 7

You may wish to cement the head of the Woolly Bugger to increase durability (optional).

©Steve Probasco

Trophy Rainbow trout from Minnie Lake, British Columbia.

Dragonfly Nymph

The Dragonfly Nymph is one of the most productive fly patterns for fishing still waters. This "meat and potatoes" insect is big, and is a staple in the trout's diet. A properly fished Dragonfly Nymph is seldom refused.

The best place to fish this nymph is in or around weed beds. Use whatever line is necessary to get your fly down into the weeds and keep it there. Retrieve the fly slowly, working it through the vegetation. Be prepared for violent takes; trout are seldom bashful when it comes to picking up one of these large morsels.

One of the Dragonfly Nymph's most outstanding features is its large eyes. The melted monofilament eyes used on this imitation do a very good job of emulating the natural.

Even during times when other insects are hatching, a big ol' Dragonfly Nymph crawled along the bottom of a lake or pond will usually put a bend in your rod.

MATERIALS

Hook: Mustad 33960 (long-shank hook)

Thread: Black

Body: Dark olive chenille

Hackle: Dark olive

Eyes: Monofilament line (40- to 60-pound-test)

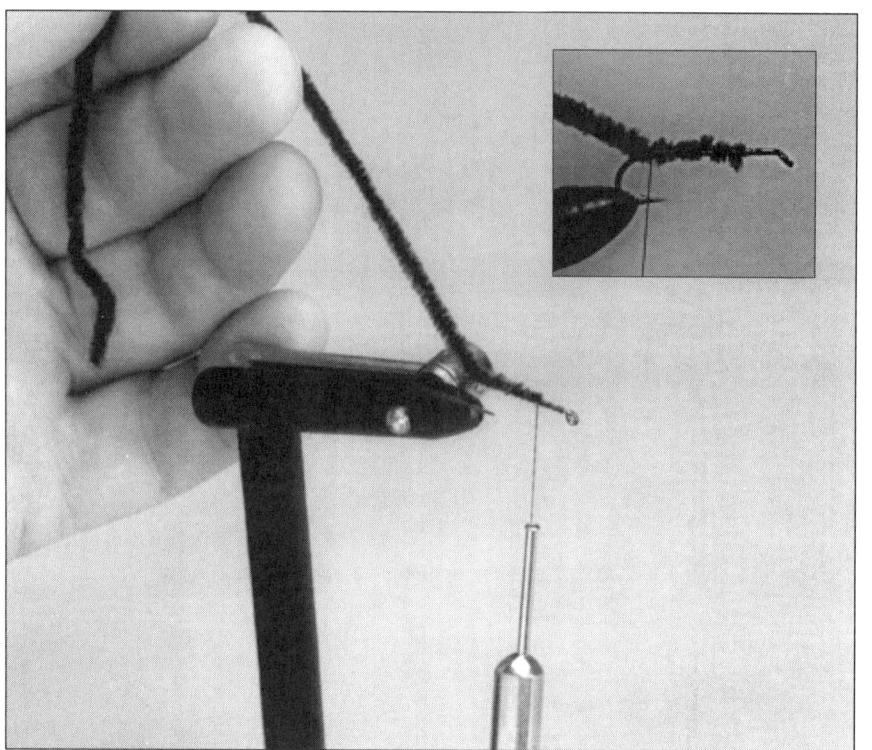

Step 1

Wrap hook shank with thread.

Starting one-third of the way down the shank, lay a 4-inch piece of chenille along the hook and secure using the soft loop technique. Wind the thread tightly around the chenille, beginning at eye end and wrapping to just above the barb.

Secure chenille with several wraps of the thread above the barb, then wind thread forward two-thirds of the way up the hook shank toward the eye.

Step 2

Wind the chenille forward tightly, two-thirds of the way up the hook shank. Secure body materials with the tying thread, wrapping to just above the barb and back up, all the way to the eye.

Carefully trim off excess chenille.

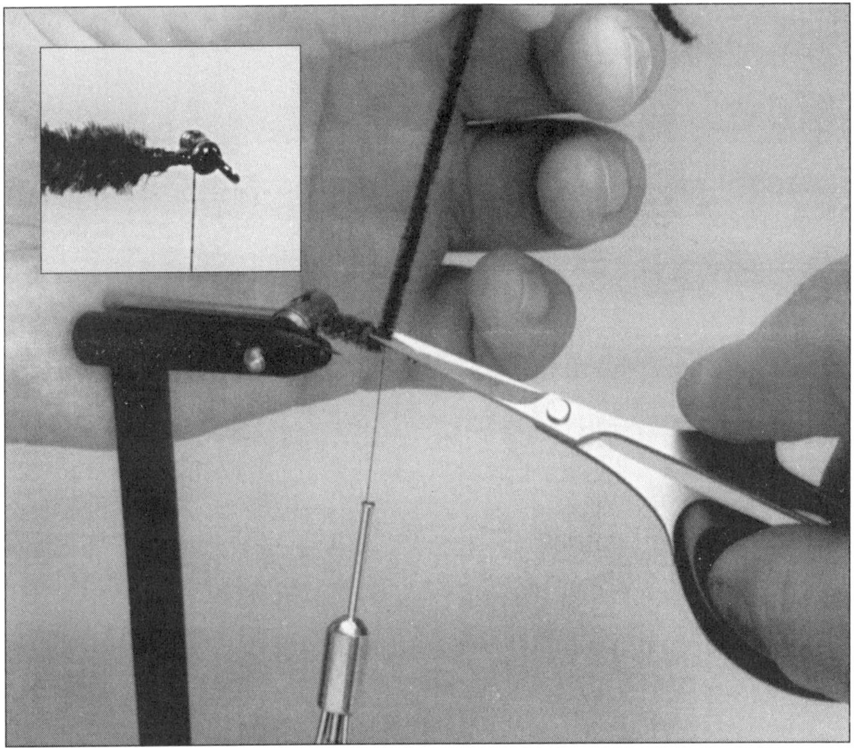

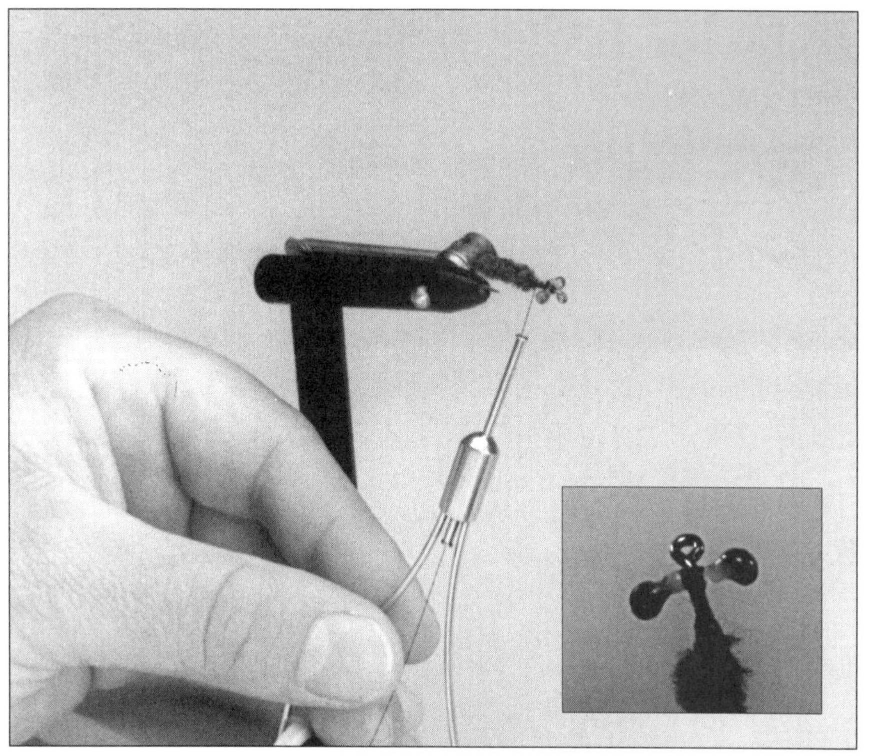

Step 3

Make a set of monofilament eyes as described earlier (see page 33).

Secure the eyes to the top of the hook using a crisscross, or figure eight, motion of the thread. Once eyes are secured, wrap thread back down to where you stopped winding the chenille up the body.

Step 4

With scissors, clip 1½ inch from the tip (not quill end) of an olive saddle hackle, and save for tying the PEACOCK SOFT HACKLE.

Tie the remaining section to the hook immediately in front of the chenille and just behind the eyes, as shown. Carefully clip any excess quill or fibers at eye end.

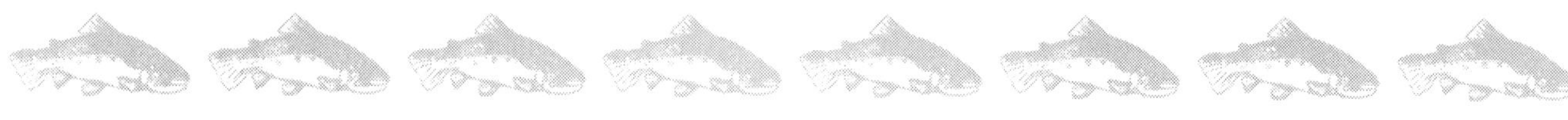

Step 5

Tie in a 2-inch piece of olive chenille in front of the hackle. Allow excess chenille to trail forward, toward eyes.

Step 6

Wind the hackle three turns in place (just behind chenille). Pull fibers and excess chenille forward with right hand and use left hand to secure hackle with the tying thread, passing bobbin over and around. Wind thread forward completely to hook eye.

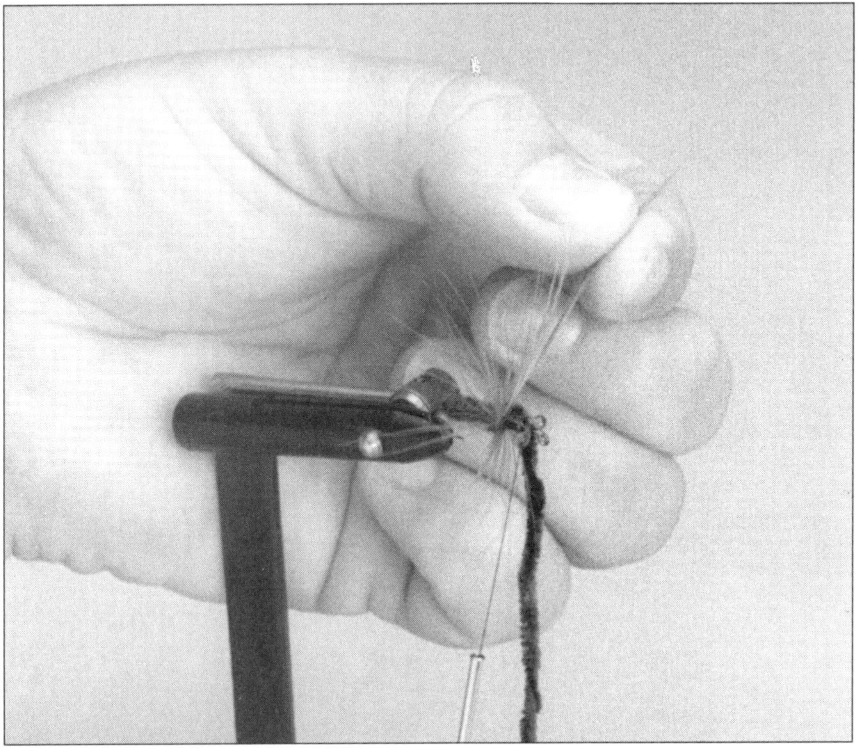

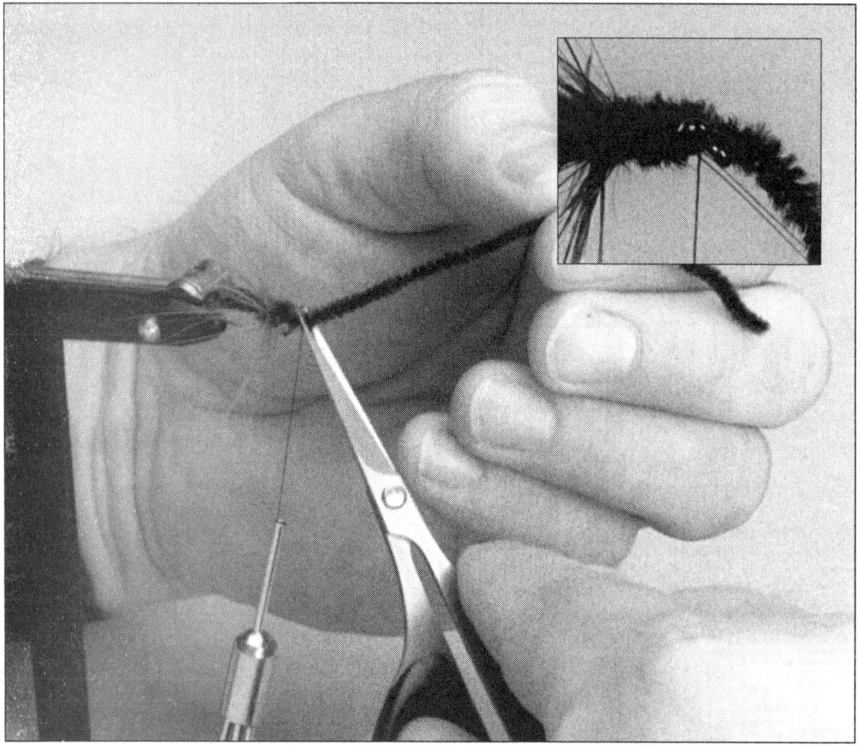

Step 7

Pull fibers back out of the way and wind the remaining chenille forward to the head, pull between the eyes, and secure with the tying thread just behind the hook eye.

Trim chenille in front of eyes and behind hook eye. Half hitch or whip finish the head.

Step 8

You may wish to apply cement to the head of the DRAGONFLY NYMPH to increase durability (optional).

Carey Special

The Carey Special is a very versatile fly pattern. Tied in a variety of sizes, it is suggestive of many different aquatic nymphs. It is an excellent "search pattern" and has proven itself many times over in all types of water and fishing situations.

This fly can be tied using a wide variety of body materials, but chenille is the all-time favorite. It can be tied in virtually every color under the sun. Brown, black, olive, green, yellow, and red are very popular. Hook sizes vary, of course, with the type of fish you are after and the kind of water being fished.

When searching new water with the Carey Special, fish it at varying depths until you locate trout. The Carey is as at home fished with a floating line in the surface film, as it is weighted and bounced along the bottom.

The standard Carey Special is a heavily hackled fly. It is sometimes beneficial to trim the hackles with nail clippers to match the naturals you find in the water, and fish it along the bottom. This will make the fly more nymphlike in appearance.

MATERIALS

Hook: 33960 (long-shank hook)

Thread: Black

Tail: Pheasant rump fibers

Body: Olive chenille

Hackle: Pheasant rump feathers

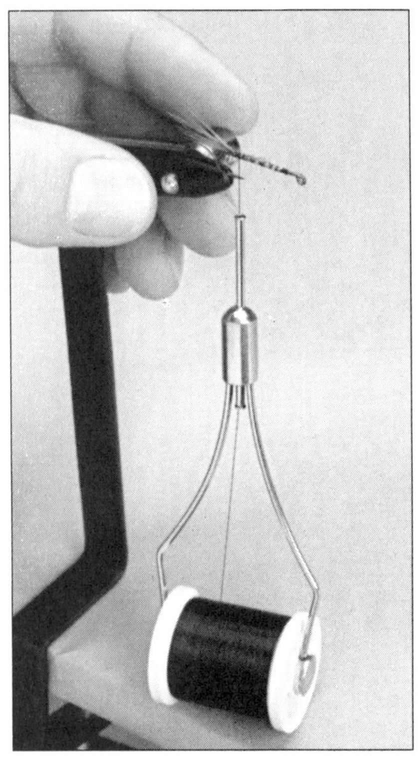

Step 1

Cover the hook with tying thread.

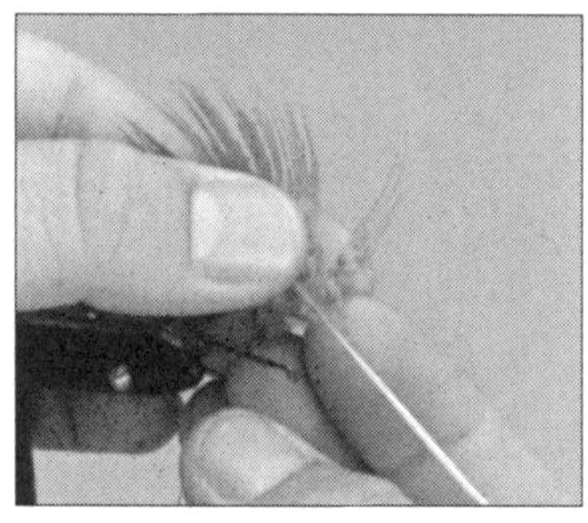

Strip about 1/4 inch of straight fibers from each side of a pheasant rump feather (just above the fuzz). Strip fuzz from quill.

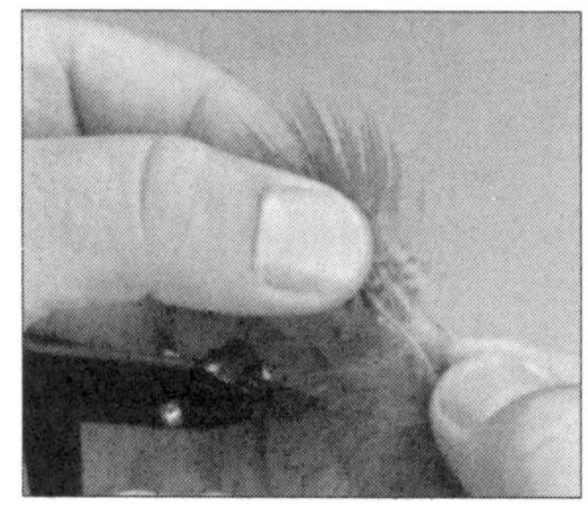

Lay along shank beginning 1/8 inch behind hook eye to extend beyond hook for a tail, as shown. Using the soft loop, secure fibers just above the barb, then wrap forward to eye and back.

Step 2

Tie in a 4-inch piece of chenille, securing it with a soft loop just above the barb and winding thread forward to the hook eye.

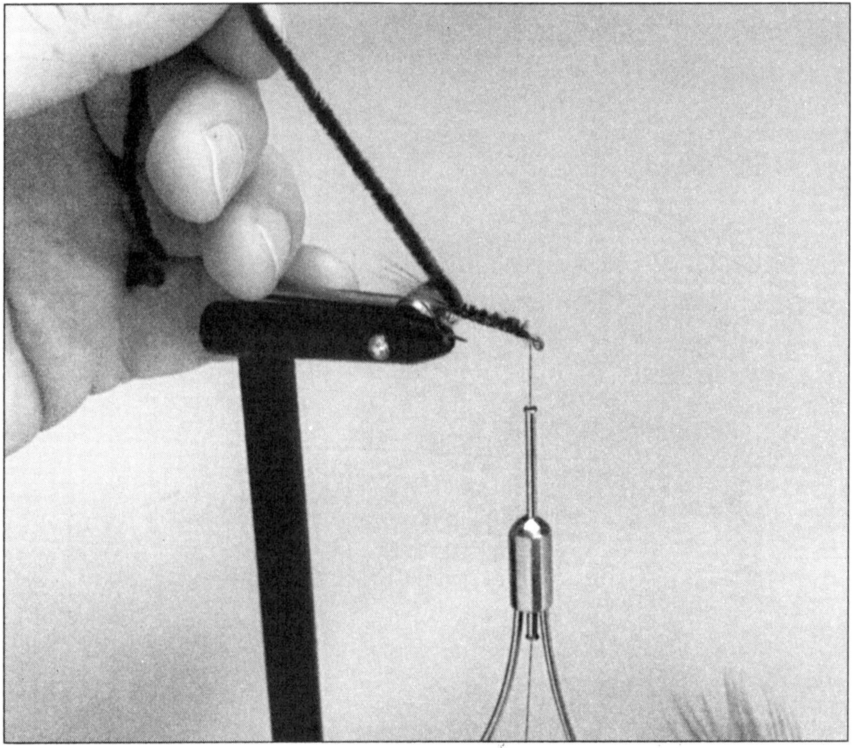

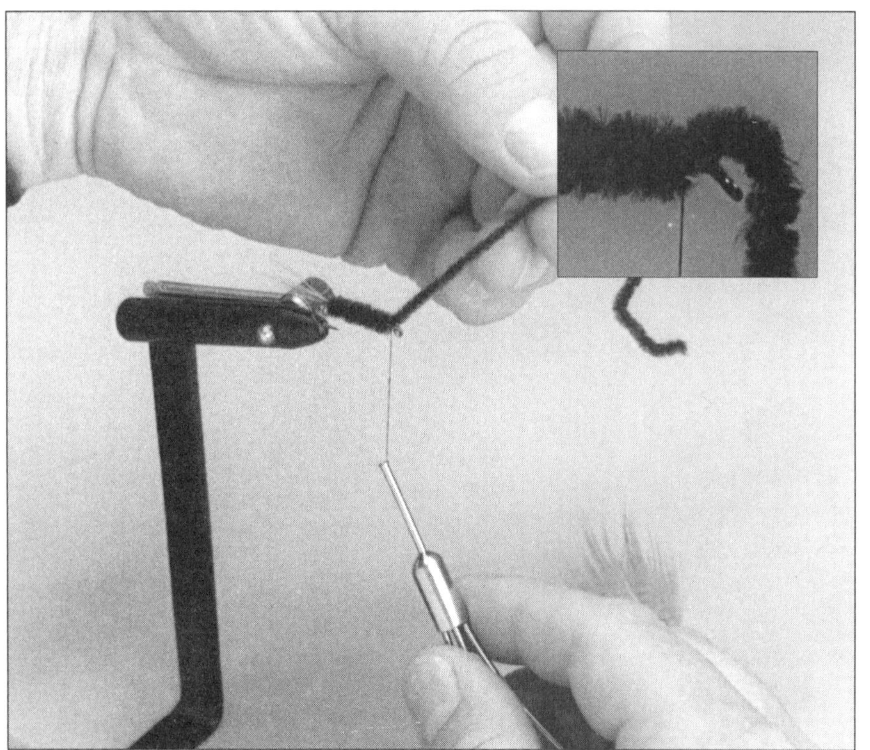

Step 3

Wind chenille forward tightly to form the body. Stop winding and secure the chenille about 1/8 inch from the eye of the hook, as shown. Secure with thread and trim.

Step 4

Secure quill end of the pheasant rump feather just in front of the chenille and behind hook eye.

Step 5

Using hackle pliers or fingers, wind hackle three or four turns in place just behind hook eye, and secure.

Pull the hackle fibers forward and hold them out of the way with your right hand.

Use left hand to bring bobbin up and over, wrapping all materials securely.

Step 6

Pull fibers back along body and wrap thread in front of them to create fly's head. Finish with a series of half hitches or whip finish head. You may cement for increased durability (optional).

Clipped Carey Special

For an alternative fly that's a good choice for imitating various nymphs, simply clip the front hackle of the CAREY SPECIAL.

©Steve Probasco

Rainbow Trout taken on a Carey Special.

Pheasant Tail Nymph

There are a few nymph patterns in existence that just work everywhere. The Pheasant Tail Nymph is one of them. This fly is one of the best mayfly nymph imitations around. In addition, it does a good job of imitating several other aquatic insects when tied in a variety of sizes.

The simplicity of this pattern is part of its beauty. It consists of only a couple of different materials. Because of the pattern's slim profile, it sinks rapidly. It can be fished at varying depths by using full-floating to full-sinking lines, and is effective at any depth trout are feeding.

Keep in mind that most nymphs move slowly through the water. Fish this fly with short strips of the fly line, and pay attention to weed beds and rocky bottoms where there are an abundance of mayfly nymphs.

MATERIALS

Hook: Mustad 3399-A (short-shank hook)

Thread: Black

Tail: Pheasant tail fibers

Abdomen: Pheasant tail fibers

Rib: Small copper wire

Thorax: Peacock herl

Wing Case: Pheasant tail fibers

Legs: Pheasant tail fibers

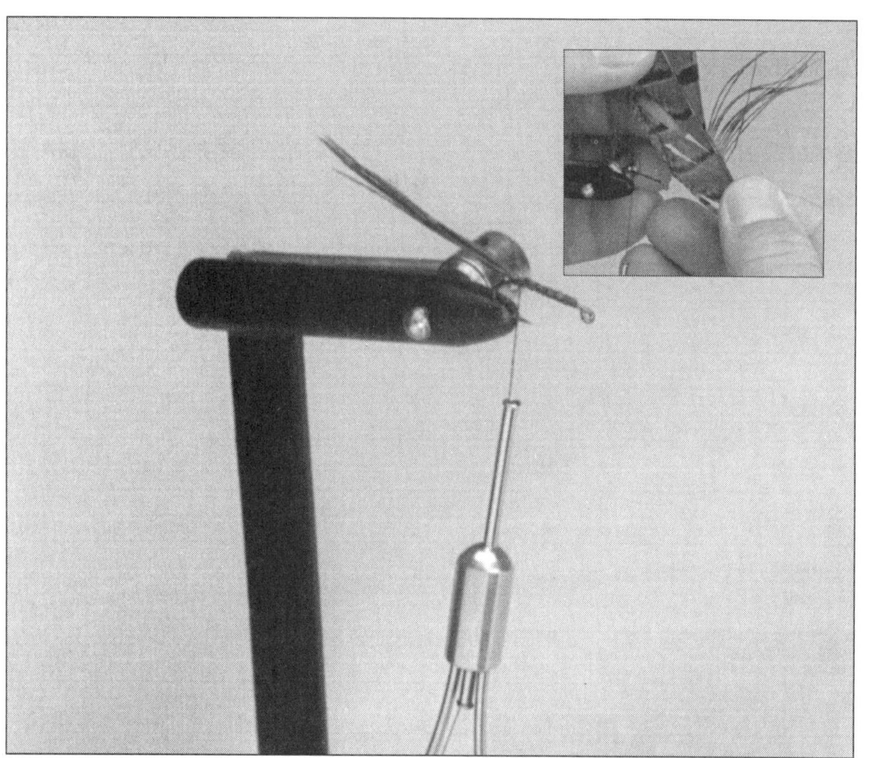

Step 1

Cover the hook with tying thread.

Strip 10 to 12 fibers about twice the length of the hook shank from the pheasant tail and lay along the hook from behind the eye. Using the soft loop, secure the fibers to the hook shank, just above the barb. Wrap the fibers on the shank tightly, from the barb to just behind the hook eye and back to barb.

Step 2

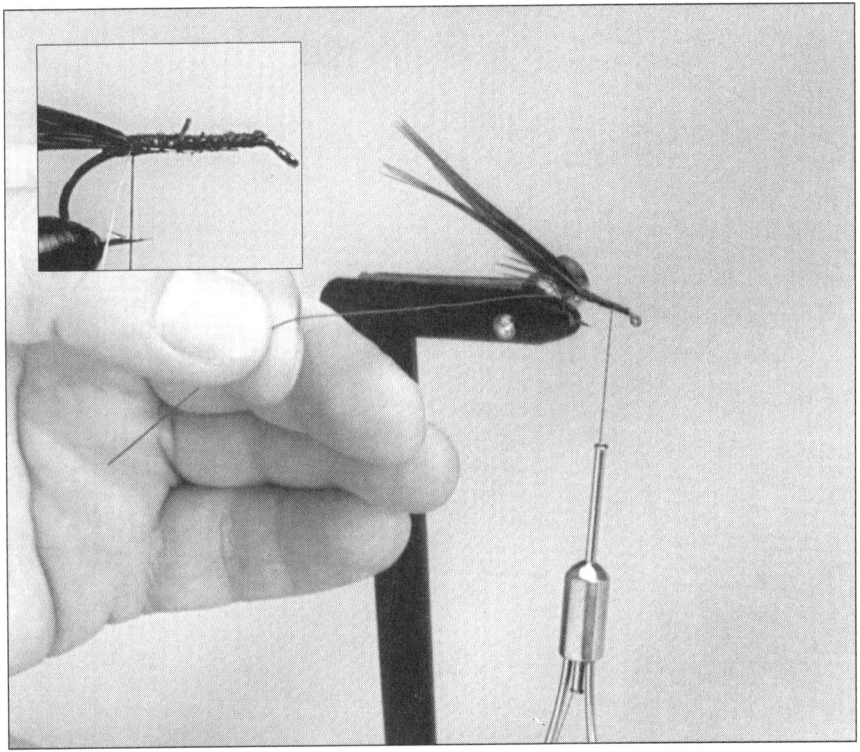

Tie in a second small section of pheasant tail (about twice the length of the hook shank) just above the barb, to extend one length beyond the original tail section.

Wrap thread forward. Secure a 4-inch piece of the wire just behind the hook eye. Lay wire along shank and wrap with thread, from eye to above barb and two-thirds of the way back up the hook shank.

Excess wire trails off at barb.

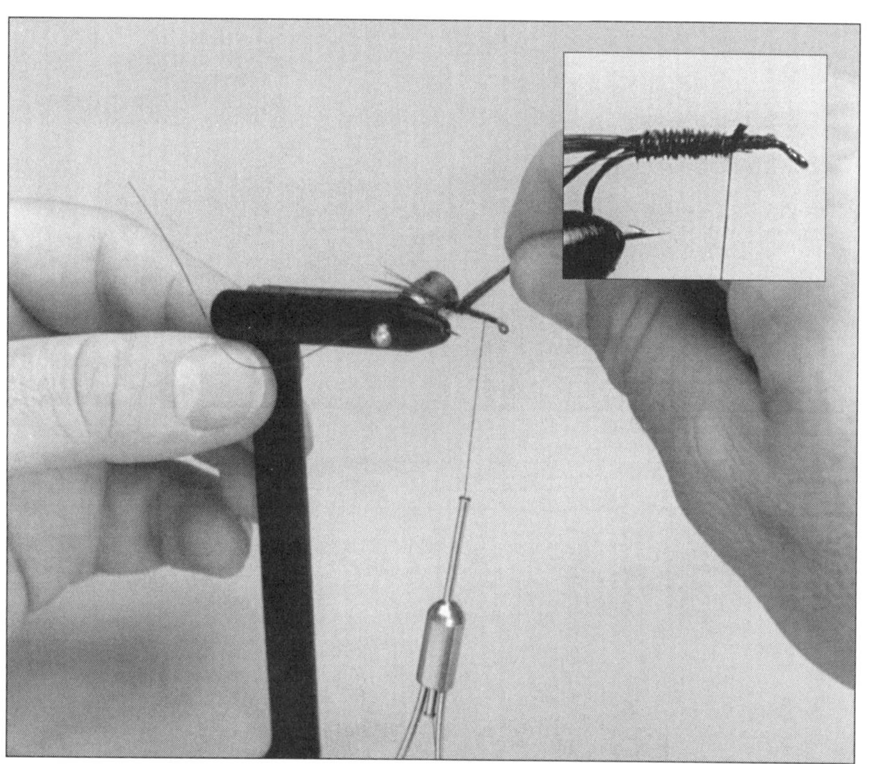

Step 3

Wind the longest pheasant tail fibers two-thirds of the way up the shank, toward the hook eye. Secure with thread at the head. Carefully clip off excess.

Step 4

Wind the wire forward in a counterclockwise direction, leaving spaces between wraps to form the rib of the fly, as shown. Secure at the same point you secured the pheasant tail, two-thirds of the way up the shank toward the hook eye.

Clip excess wire.

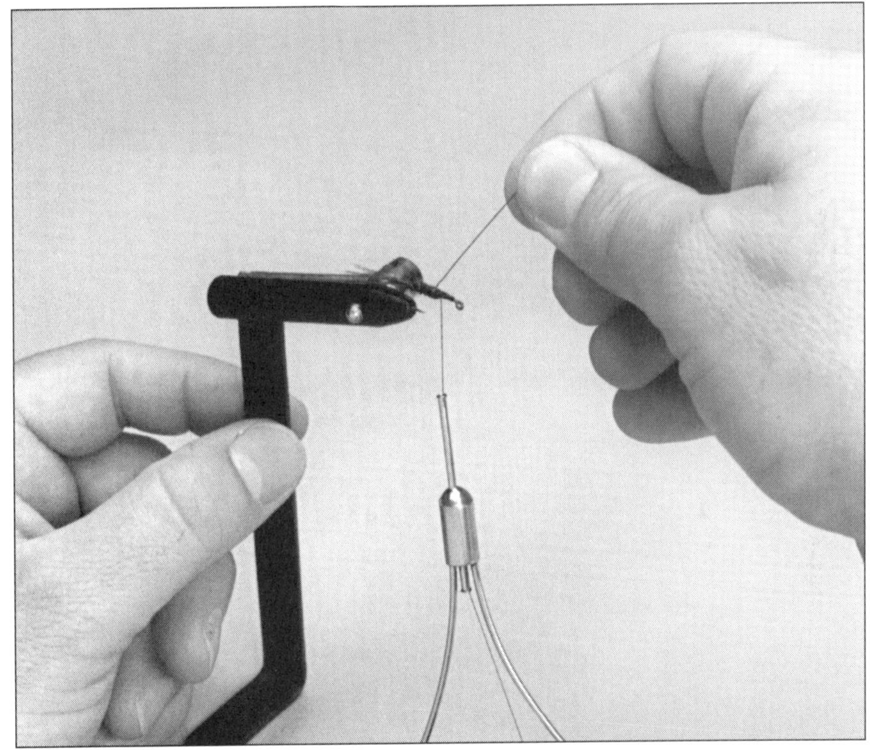

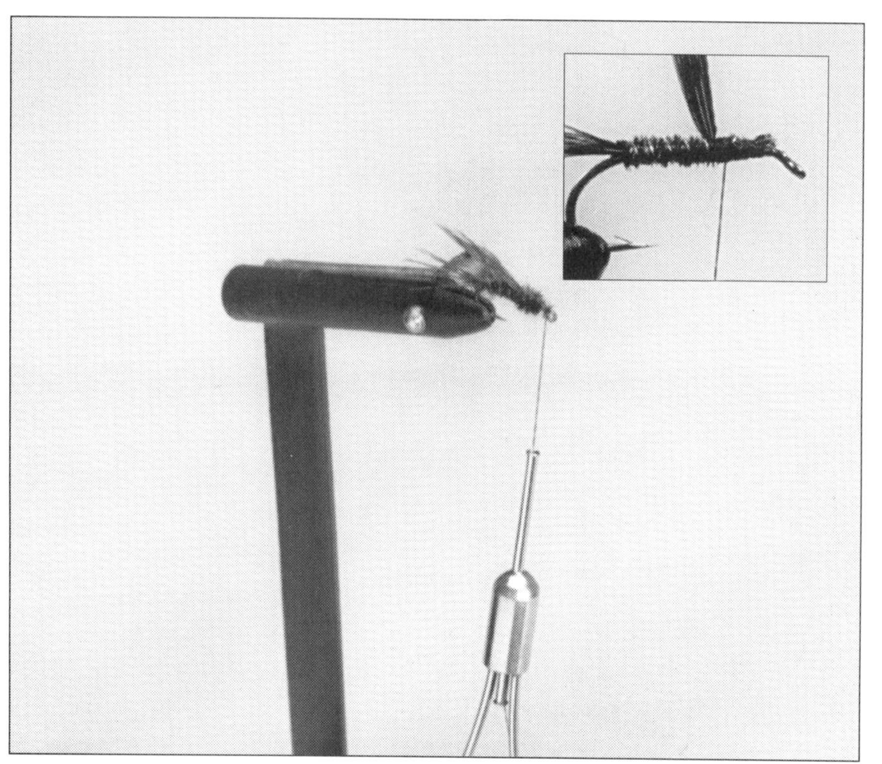

Step 5

Use a soft loop to tie in another section of 10 to 12 pheasant tail fibers where you clipped the wire (two-thirds the way up the hook shank). These fibers should be the length of the hook from eye to furthest reach of the bend. They will become the fly's wing case and legs.

Step 6

Tie in three strands of peacock herl just in front of the wing case, as shown. Trim any excess hurl at short end and wind thread forward to hook eye. Allow the long ends of the herl to trail off the body in front of the wings.

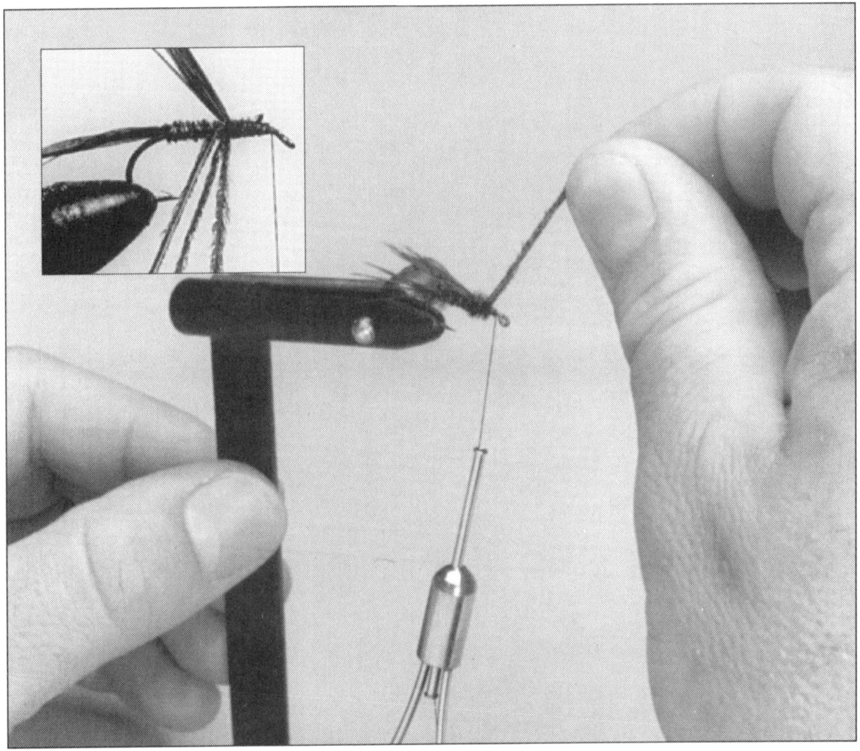

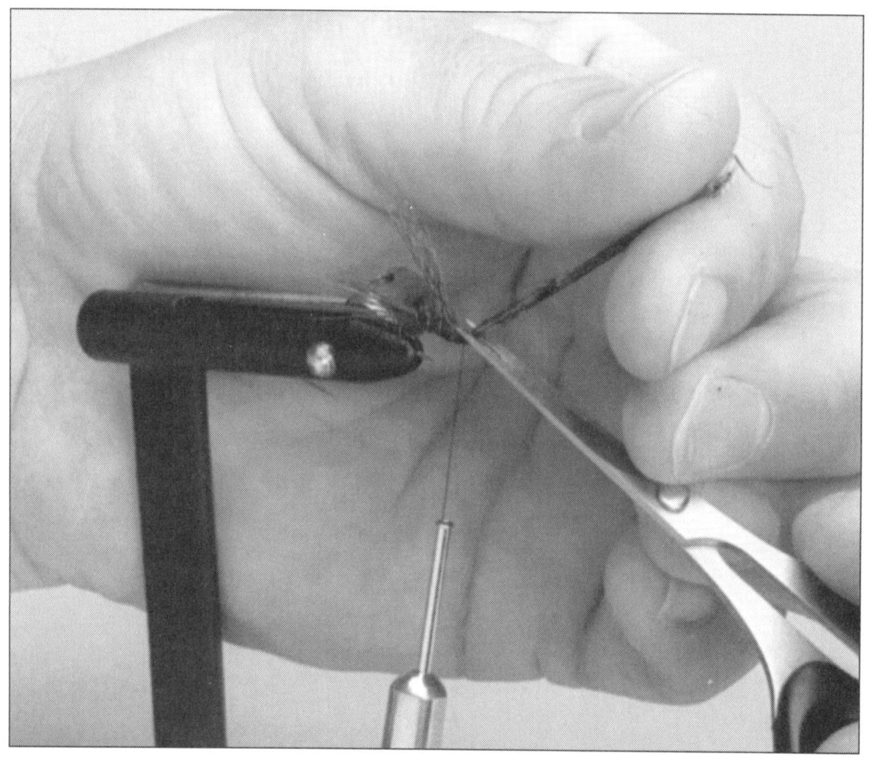

Step 7

Tightly wind all three strands of the peacock herl forward to the head of the fly and secure with thread. Clip off excess.

Step 8

Pull the pheasant tail fibers acting as wing case forward. Secure fibers atop the peacock herl with three turns of the tying thread at the point just behind the hook eye. This will form the wing case.

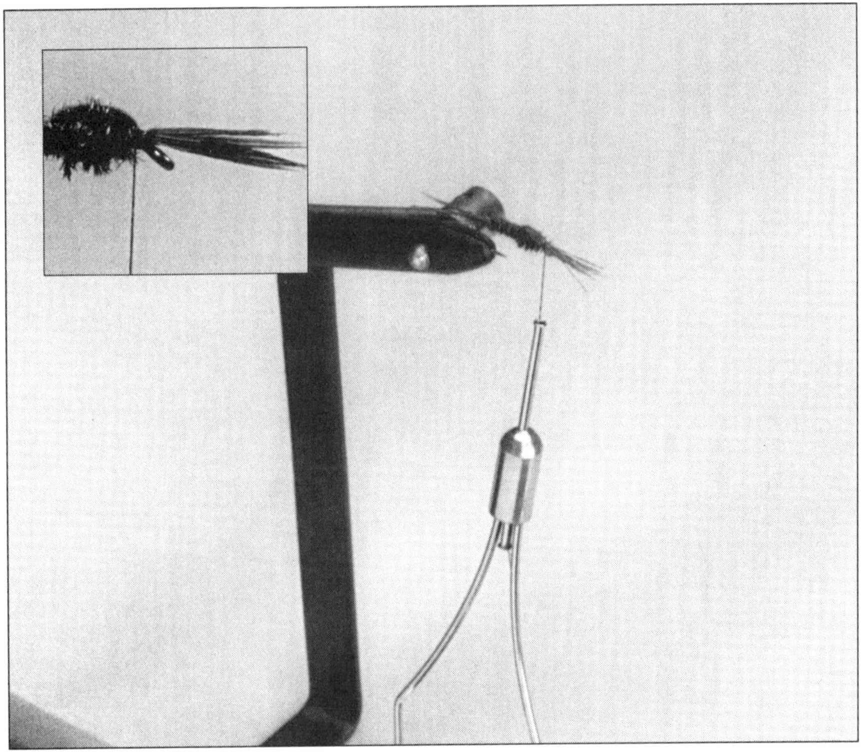

Step 9

Separate the pheasant fibers now extended in front of the hook eye into two equal bunches and pull backwards along each side of the fly. Hold in place with the fingers of your left hand.

Use your right hand to wrap the tying thread tightly behind the hook eye, simultaneously forming the head of the fly and securing the legs along the side of the body.

Step 10

Finish head with a series of half hitches. Cement the head if desired.

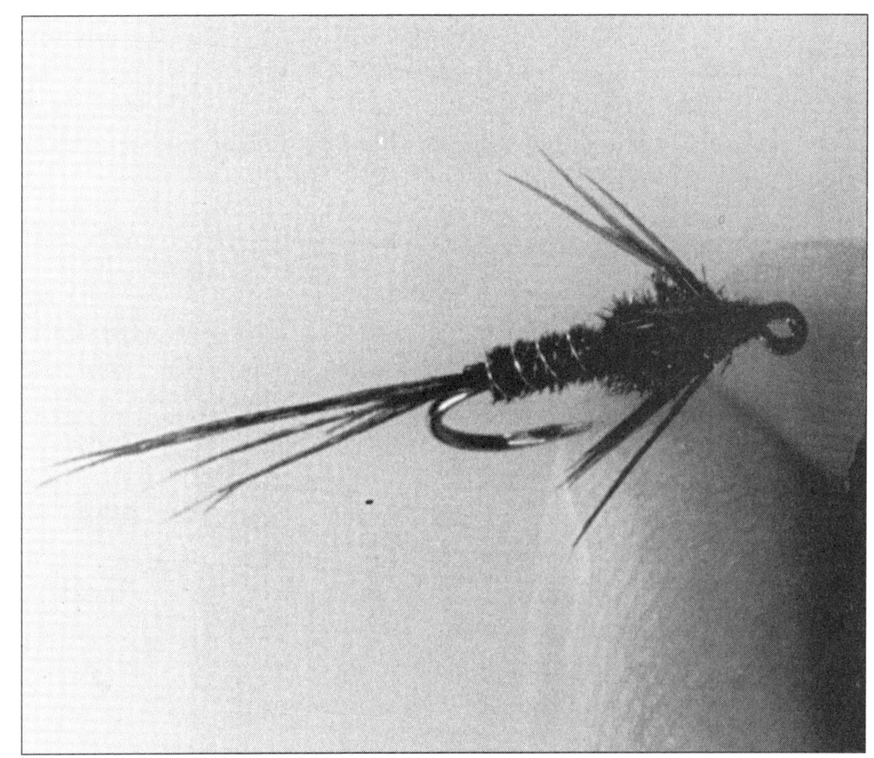

Peacock Soft Hackle

There are times when attempting to match a hatch exactly just doesn't pan out. All of the flies that should work...don't! It is possible during these times that the fish are taking emerging insects, rather than the visible ones. When this is the case, there is no fly better than a soft hackle.

A soft-hackled fly generally resembles the pupal stage of many different insects. The long, soft hackle fibers pulsate as the fly is drawn through the water, resembling the emerging insect as it swims to the surface.

The Peacock Soft Hackle resembles the drab coloration of many aquatic insects. This is a good fly to use over weed beds, where you should slowly work the fly to the surface. It is also very effective when using the standard down-and-across approach: you cast out slightly downstream and let the line swing with the current. This draws the fly to the surface as the line completes the swing. As the fly rises, it is very vulnerable.

MATERIALS

Hook: Mustad 3399-A (short-shank hook)

Body: Peacock herl

Rib: Copper wire

Hackle: Olive hackle tip

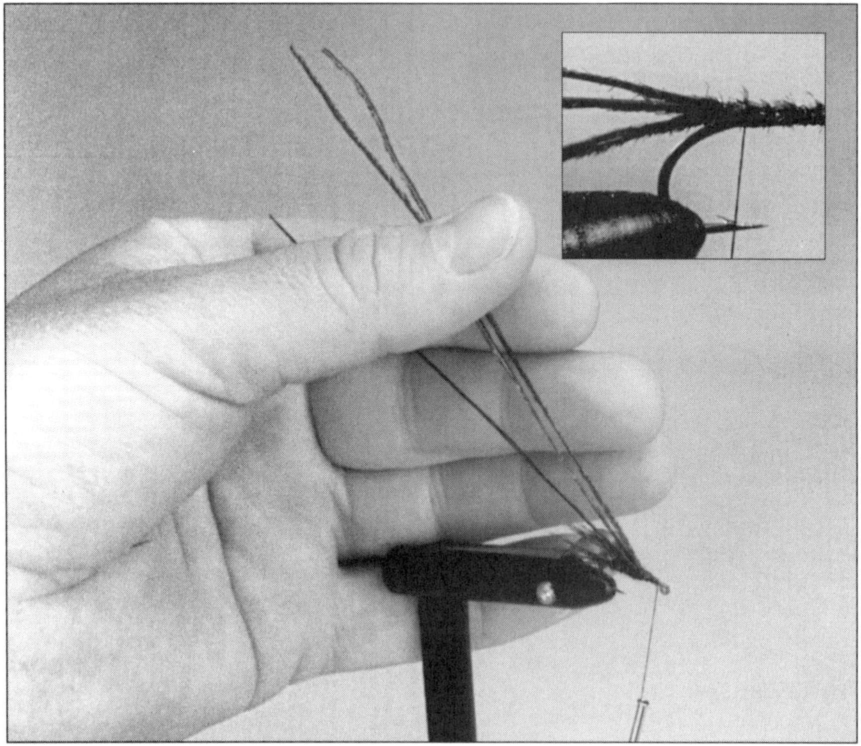

Tying Steps

Step 1

Cover the hook shank with tying thread. Use a soft loop to secure five strands of peacock herl on the shank directly behind the hook eye.

Trim any herl that extends forward of securing point.

Lay long strands of herl along shank and wrap with thread to directly above the barb.

Step 2

Wind thread forward and tie in a 3-inch piece of copper wire from the eye to the barb, as with the herl in Step 1.

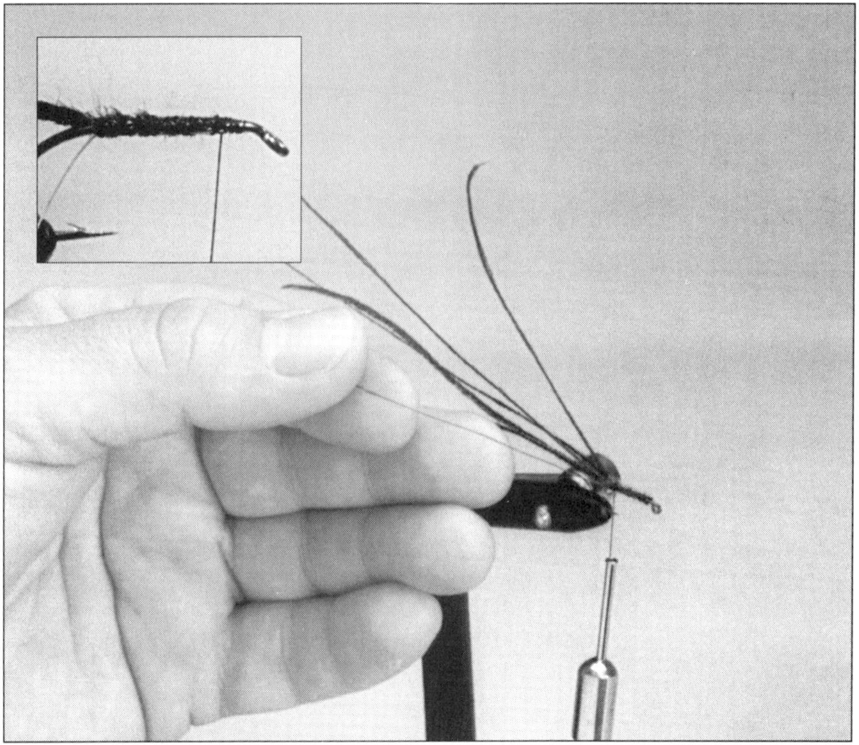

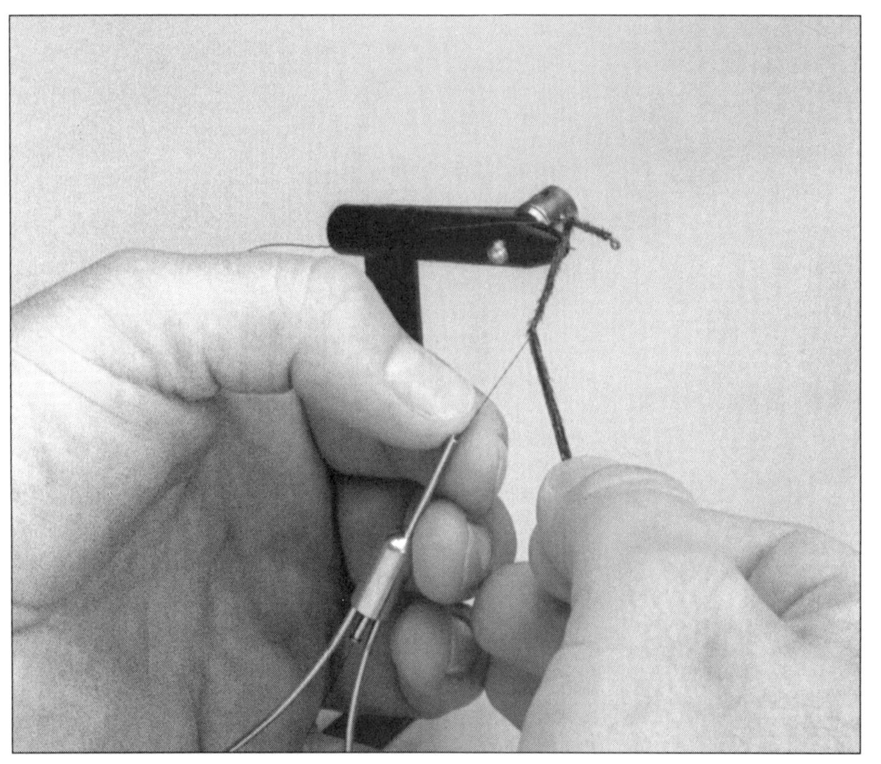

Step 3

Wind the peacock herl tightly around 2 inches of the tying thread, leading off the barb end of the shank, as shown.

Step 4

Wind the herl-wrapped thread forward to the eye of the hook. Free the tying thread and secure the herl to the hook just behind the eye.

Trim excess herl.

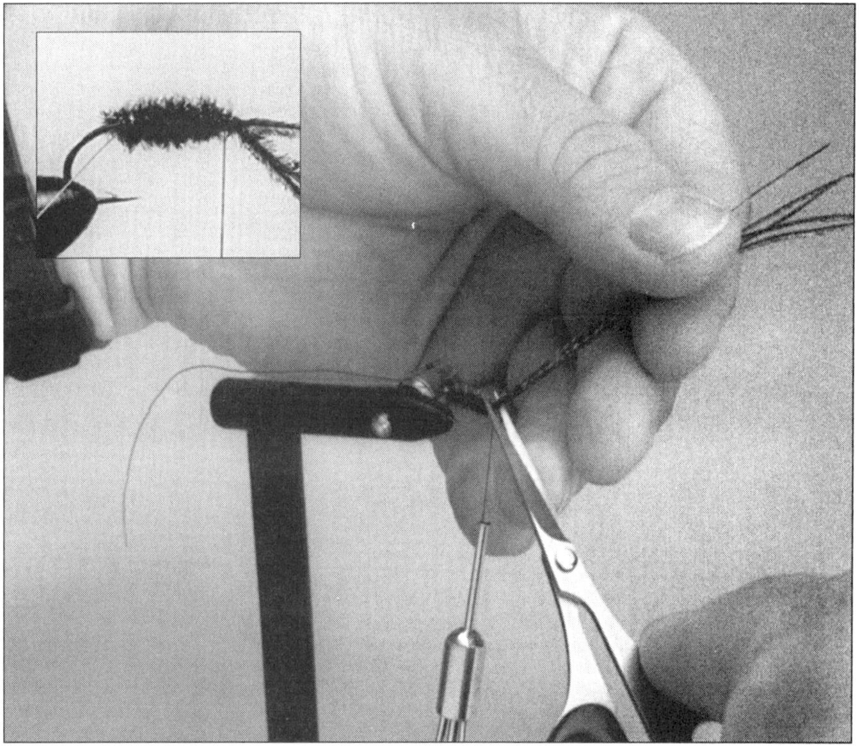

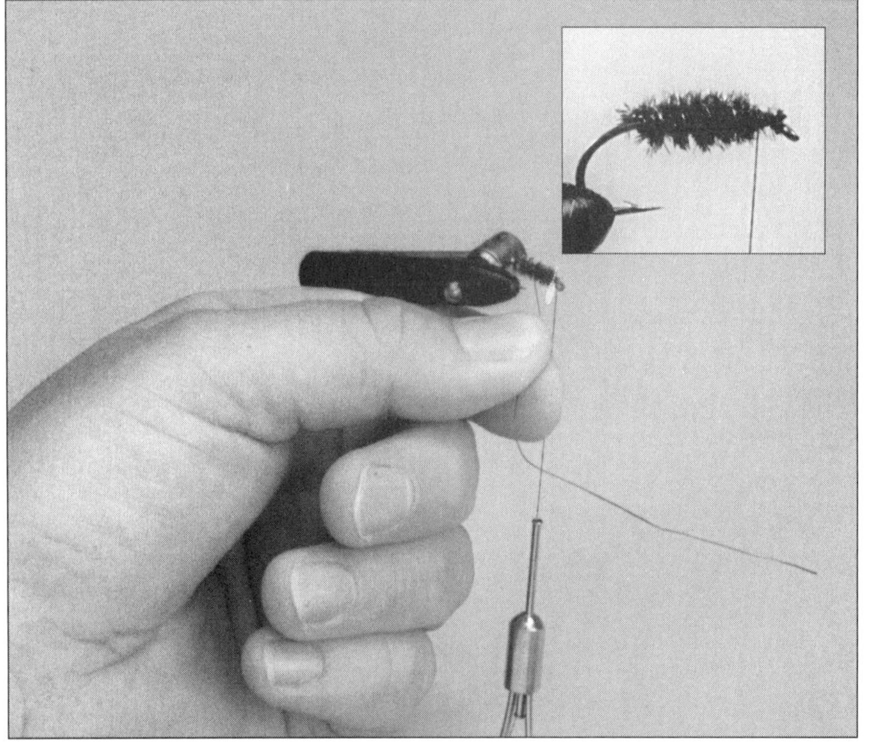

Step 5

Wind the wire forward counterclockwise over the peacock herl, leaving even spaces between ribs. Secure with wrapping thread at the head and trim excess wire.

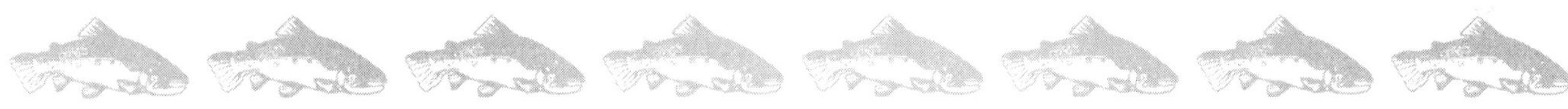

Step 6

Tie in the quill end of the hackle tip left over from tying the DRAGONFLY NYMPH (see page 55) just behind the hook eye, as shown.

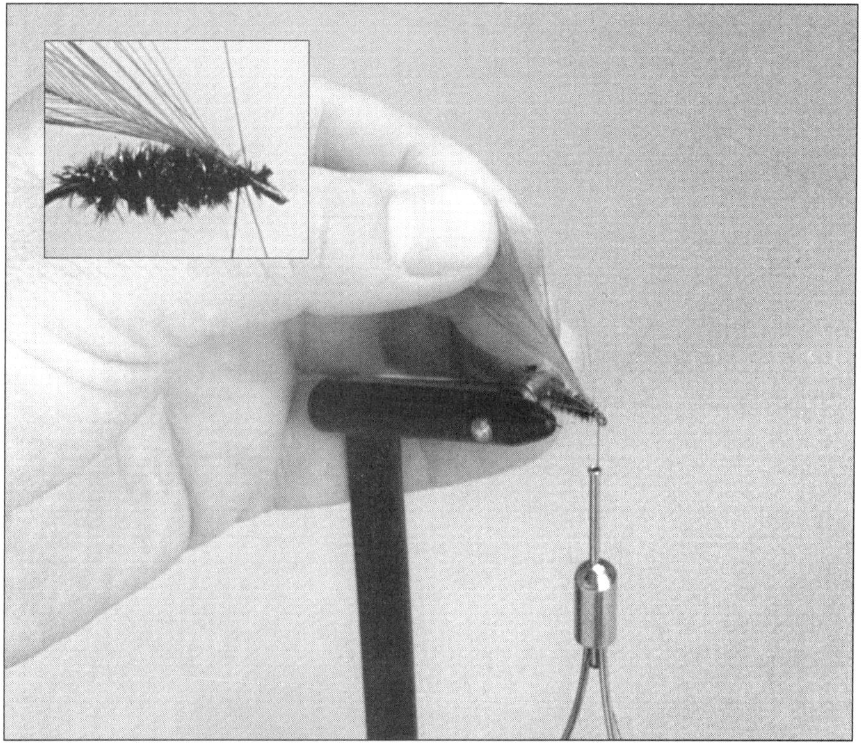

Step 7

Attach the hackle pliers to tip of feather and wind the hackle two or three turns in one place, just behind the hook eye and in front of the body. Secure with thread and clip excess hackle extending in front of the point where it's tied in.

Step 8

Pull hackle back out of the way and wind on a head.

Use a series of half hitches or the whip finisher to tie off the head. Cement if you choose.

Afterword

At this point you have learned several basic fly-tying procedures and techniques. You now know the basics for tying on various materials to create different styles of flies. What you have learned from tying the five flies featured—Woolly Bugger, Dragonfly Nymph, Carey Special, Pheasant Tail Nymph, and Peacock Soft Hackle—will enable you to tie a host of other popular patterns.

All you need to do now is buy more materials, maybe a few more tools, get a more advanced book on fly tying—one that demonstrates how to tie a pile of flies—and you're in business. Advanced procedures will be much easier now that you have the basics down.

The more you learn about fly tying, the more you will get into entomology, and the more creative and realistic your flies will become. In fact, tying flies to imitate the naturally occurring foods of the fish you are after will become as fun as catching the fish. Well, almost!

As I mentioned, with the skills you have already learned, you are now able to tie a variety of useful flies and start filling up fly boxes.

Following is a list of productive fly patterns you can now tie with your newly acquired skills.

GRAY HACKLE YELLOW

Hook: Standard length, sizes 14 to 6
Thread: Black
Body: Yellow or gold floss
Rib: Medium gold Mylar
Tail: Scarlet hackle fibers
Hackle: Grizzly, tied bushy

ZUG BUG

Hook: Standard length, sizes 18 to 6
Thread: Black
Tail: Peacock herl (three fibers trimmed short)
Body: Three or four peacock herl fibers
Rib: Small copper wire or Mylar
Wing Case: Turkey quill
Hackle: Brown hackle fibers, tied as beard

WOOLLY WORM

Hook: Heavy wire, 2X long, sizes 14 to 4
Thread: Black
Tail: Red hackle fibers
Body: Chenille (black, olive, red, brown, yellow)
Hackle: Grizzly saddle

CADDIS EMERGER

Hook: Standard length, sizes 16 to 8
Thread: Black
Body: Tan, cream, green, or brown wool (match the color of the emergers found in your fishing water)
Hackle: Partridge (one turn)
Head: Two strands of black ostrich herl

CADDIS LARVA

Hook: Standard length, sizes 16 to 8
Thread: Black
Body: Tan, cream, green, or brown wool
Head: Black ostrich herl

MARABOU LEECH

Hook: 2X or 3X long, sizes 10 to 2
Thread: Black
Tail: Black marabou
Body: Black marabou
Wing: Black marabou

NYERGES NYMPH

Hook: 2X long, sizes 14 to 8
Thread: Black
Body: Dark olive chenille
Hackle: Brown, palmered, and clipped off top of fly

PARTRIDGE & ORANGE SOFT HACKLE

Hook: Standard length, sizes 16 to 10
Thread: Orange
Body: Orange floss
Hackle: Brown partridge

RED HACKLE

Hook: Standard length, sizes 14 to 10
Thread: Black
Rib: Small gold tinsel or Mylar
Body: Peacock herl
Hackle: Red furnace

Suggested Reading

Borger, Gary. *Designing Trout Flies*. Wausau, WI: Tomorrow River Press, 1991.

Hughes, Dave. *American Fly Tying Manual*. Portland, OR: Frank Amato Publications, 1992.

Morris, Skip. *Fly Tying Made Clear and Simple*. Portland, OR: Frank Amato Publications, 1992.

Steve Probasco is an award-winning, full-time outdoor writer/photographer living in Raymond, Washington. He specializes in fly-fishing, and his "research" takes him all over North America. Probasco's articles and photographs appear regularly in several regional, national, and international publications. He is the author of five fly-fishing books and one video on fly tying.